.

TOO STUPID
TO FAIL

**WHY THE RESILIENT WILL ALWAYS
BEAT THE INTELLIGENT**

DR. STEPHEN CRAWFORD

ARCHWAY
PUBLISHING

Archway Publishing books may be ordered through booksellers or by contacting:

Archway Publishing
1663 Liberty Drive
Bloomington, IN 47403
www.archwaypublishing.com
844-669-3957

Because of the dynamic nature of the Internet, any web addresses or links contained in this book may have changed since publication and may no longer be valid. The views expressed in this work are solely those of the author and do not necessarily reflect the views of the publisher, and the publisher hereby disclaims any responsibility for them.

ISBN: 978-1-6657-1477-8 (sc)
ISBN: 978-1-6657-1476-1 (hc)
ISBN: 978-1-6657-1478-5 (e)

Library of Congress Control Number: 2021922306

Print information available on the last page.

Archway Publishing rev. date: 11/20/2021

CONTENTS

PART I: THE BATTLE OF THE HEAD

PART II: THE BATTLE OF THE HEART

PART III: THE BATTLE OF THE HANDS

FOREWORD BY
DR. JOSEPH MCCLENDON III

We live in exciting times where there has been an explosion in new information from books, social media, and podcasts. Our world is inundated with exploration, research, and major findings in scientific inquiry. The geologist is studying the earth and its history; the astronomer is exploring the great expanse of our universe; but who studies the deeper mysteries of human potential? This feat is left to those of us who dare to go into the unknown and discover that the greatest mysteries in the universe lie within us. I am, by education, a neuropsychologist, and by trade, I'm an Ultimate Performance Specialist, which simply means I help people get the best out of themselves. I have spent the first part of my career training and encouraging people to see what is possible when it comes to their potential. It is in these most recent years that I have made the commitment to mentor and activate leaders who can carry on the legacy of launching people into the next level of their genius. I chose to write the foreword for this book because Stephen is one of the bold few that I have selected to mentor and pour myself into during this season of my career to raise up an army of world changers. Stephen has joined with me as we quietly build an army of Neuroencoders to help reprogram the way people think.

And I think what's most important is what Stephen already brings to the table. He is an outstanding leader, mentor, visionary, And business professional that has impacted the lives of thousands and thousands in their endeavors to go further faster in their lives. Along with his amazing communication and impact skills he brings the heart of a true champion leads with compassion and love for those that he influences. Didn't take long for me or for that matter, anybody to recognize that Stephen has something special and he's driven to share his gifts with others.

My mentor Jim Rohn used to say, "Formal education will make you a living, but self-education will make you a fortune." For what it's worth, most people don't really know how to get out of their own way when it comes to successful living. The reason I love this book is because Stephen tackles this subject head on and doesn't pull any punches. When I wrote my first book it was out of this same sense of curiosity that Stephen demonstrates in his book. He starts with the premise that we are all created equal, yet not all of us share in the opportunity of that equality, and rather than spending the time wallowing in the problem, he starts right away introducing us to solutions. I've often taught and at times fell victim to 'Imposter Syndrome'.

Imposter Syndrome is the feeling that you are not who you say you are, or you are not deserving of the opportunities presented to you, of the skills you possess, or a general inability to live up to the reputation you have. With Imposter Syndrome, you may assume that people don't respect you or think very highly of you – almost as though they can "see through" you. I remember a time when I never used to mention my doctorate because it wasn't from what some used to refer to as a "prestigious" university. So rather than be proud and celebrate the hard work I did, I simply felt like an imposter, especially in the academic world, for instance, while teaching at UCLA. It's a shame how common this is, and it all boils down to a lack of personal integrity. Imposter Syndrome emerges from an internal battle between who you really are and what you think you're supposed to be. This is distinctly different than having goals and aspirations you're working toward but instead may present itself by making excuses like, "If only I had this type of education…" or "If only I had started this sooner, I'd be much better off..." None of this is serving who you are now OR who you'd like to become.

The framework that Stephen lays out gives you 9 checkpoints to reflect on that serve almost as guideposts for moving away from the fears and self-doubt that limit our success and mass-produce mediocrity. He teaches you how to grow the muscles that give you staying power. I would definitely say that after three decades in an industry where most burn out after one year that I have learned a thing or two about staying power.

The three battles that everyone must fight – the battle of the head, the heart, and the hands – are simple, but don't let their simplicity fool you. Just because something is simple doesn't mean that it doesn't virtually remain a mystery. And make no mistake about it, any truth that lacks awareness remains in-actionable.

I want to make one thing clear: each person is capable of tapping into his or her own potential. Although the journey to explore and realize your potential is free, it comes at a cost. There is a hidden quality, if you will, that drives us to keep exploring while most others give up, and I daresay that this is the missing ingredient. It is through this journey that most discover the opportunity to expand, to grow, and to become the person that achieves the thing. But the becoming is the boot camp and strength training to develop the muscles required. The central thesis of this book is something I have written and spoken on for years. This idea behind moving and failing forward requires quite a bit of tenacity. While it's expected we all have different iterations of what 'tenacity' means to us, it can be reduced down to two complementary meanings.

When I met Stephen, it was in the context of the Neuroencoding program that I designed in order to help speakers, coaches, and trainers to develop the skill of not only delivering good information to people but to prepare those people for transformation. Most people believe that their challenges are based somehow on their actions while in fact they are operating based on a program that my Neuroencoders have been trained and certified to reprogram in the lives of people.I have trained Stephen and his colleagues to deliver this content and technology that I have used for over three decades to change and transform lives. By education I am a neuropsychologist; by career I am a speaker and a high-performance life coach; but my passion for years has lain in empowering everyday individuals to benefit from these modalities that for years have been limited to the very wealthy. Stephen and his confreres make this dream possible, and for that I am eternally grateful.

After my first conversation with Stephen, I knew that he would be a great fit to be on my faculty and a trainer within my program. His passion to serve people convinced me that we are kindred spirits. As I stated in my book *Unlimited Power: A Black Choice,* a work I penned with my good friend Anthony Robbins, I have long sought to elevate many of these teachings to people in the black community, and it does my heart good to see this black man carrying that same mantel in the way he lives and serves. You will truly be empowered after reading this book and be able to put many ideas into practice that will break the code to push forward and to go further faster. I wish you well as you embark on a journey that will change your life.

Let me add: "Life is exactly what you *dare* to make it, and fortune favors the bold."

JM3

INTRODUCTION

Now with God's help, I shall become myself.
—**Soren Kierkegaard**[1]

Have you ever felt trapped in your own skin? It is terrible to wake up and realize that you have freedom, but only in the way a prisoner has freedom. A prisoner can choose whether or not to eat, whether or not to sleep, and whether or not to comply with the system designed to manage their behaviors. For you, however, the place you live, the type of food you eat, and how much you must comply with a system controlled by psychological, emotional, and financial realities that are out of your control—it's all really up to you.

Yet many of us live lives similar to convicts: we make choices that are limited at best. We may choose whether we will work, we may choose what programming to watch on television, we may even choose our associates, but all these choices remain micro-decisions compared to the greatness our lives could be if we could be ourselves.

True freedom comes when a person is on a life path they designed themself. As the motivational speaker Earl Nightingale said:

> We are at our very best, and we are happiest, when we are fully engaged in work we enjoy on the journey toward the goal we've established for ourselves. It gives meaning to our time off and comfort to our

sleep. It makes everything else in life so wonderful, so worthwhile.[2]

This type of freedom gives us control over our lives while placing us in circumstances where there is ironically very little control over our future.

Let me explain. The future is predictable and controllable when we lack freedom. As someone who lacks freedom, a slave or an inmate has few choices. This lack of freedom translates into little or no opportunity to bring about change in their life.

When we choose freedom and design our own path, surprisingly, the future becomes unpredictable because the future possibilities become endless. We can choose to keep along the same path, make slight changes, or make drastic changes.

If you say yes to the freedom of designing your own life path, you can learn to let go of your inhibitions that trap you in fear or uncertainty or the snare of others' opinions. By choosing the freedom of designing your own journey, you can experience the joy of fulfillment. To experience the height of your passion, while being remunerated in a way that provides for your future, this is freedom!

In contrast, society has created a social dynamic through schools, jobs, and civic authorities that molds people into mediocre norms. Most of us in these norms are waiting for someone or something to validate us so we can become our true selves, what we already know we are. When no one opens that door for us, we stay conformed to what society expects. Society only expects us to be a shell of what we could be. But in this book, I am giving you permission to open the door to your true self and the freedom that goes with it. Abiding by a social contract that expects you to be polite and play niceties limits your growth and development. Those who play all-out are considered rude and insensitive, and we are not trained to be that way. Well, I am inviting you on a journey to live all-out.

Before we step through that door, there are some important confessions I want to make to show you that my road to self-expression was a complicated journey. These confessions are meant to fortify you for your journey if it happens to become complicated.

Confession 1: I am not that book smart.

I did well in school early on, but after fifth grade, the message I received was that I was average on the intellectual scale. I didn't do well at the game of "read, remember, and repeat." I found more excitement in connecting with people than in figuring out algebraic equations. There may have been times I surprised myself by getting a decent grade in a difficult class, but, truthfully, most of my grades throughout school were average. Nevertheless, for the larger part of the past thirty-five years, I have been in some form of schooling—though I've spent much of that time trying to figure out what most of the teachers were talking about.

I noticed that throughout school, the smart students were given great marks, honors, and recognition—they were successful in that realm. That left me with the impression that somehow the smart people would all have successful careers, but professional experience has taught me that, in the business world, nothing could be further from the truth.

This is not to say that schooling isn't important. To complete courses and years of study and to earn degrees shows that you have discipline and character, that you have what it takes to finish something.

However, to quote the late Dr. Myles Munroe: "When purpose is not known, abuse is inevitable."[4] Abuse is a construct of two words, "abnormal" and "use." In that way, I think educators are misleading their students by overpromising what grades can do for their future while undervaluing what thinking does. The purpose of education is not to teach you what to think but how to think. The greatest mistake in education is to let students believe a superior ability to learn will somehow equate to future career and financial successes.

Most of the people I coach to improve their businesses are not missing intellectual capacity; they simply use their intellectual and analytical abilities to stop themselves from doing commonsense things that would help them achieve great results. To rectify this misdirection, this book steps away from the endless theories about what "could" make you successful. Instead, it targets simple, practical habits that will move you toward success much faster than daydreaming about success ever could. If there are two secrets I want to give you in this book about how to achieve more in work and in life, they are to stop using your intellect to daydream and to stop making excuses for not changing your thought patterns.

Confession 2: I am a marshmallow eater.

Dr. Walter Mischel of Stanford University did a study that is now popularly known as the marshmallow test.[5] Children, four and five years old, were put into a room with a marshmallow on a table. They were told they had two options: They could eat the one marshmallow right away or wait for the man to come back into the room and give them a second marshmallow—and then they could eat both marshmallows. These children were being tested to see if they could practice the art of delayed gratification. What happened? After the man stepped out of the room, the majority of the children gobbled down that marshmallow faster than they could process the potential opportunity.

The test split the group in two, and Dr. Mischel named the two groups "delayers" and "grabbers." Next, for almost two decades, Mischel tracked and evaluated these children. Those who practiced delayed gratification (the delayers) scored an average of 210 points higher on the SAT. Companion studies were done and, on average, the delayers also went to better schools and achieved more lucrative careers. Unfortunately, those who ate the marshmallow right away (the grabbers) had a higher arrest rate, a lower graduation rate, and more trouble finding gainful employment on average. So, there you have it. With a penny treat, we can predict who, at the age of four, will later go to prison and who will go on to be president.

I have to be honest and say if I had been given the test when I was four years old, I would not have waited for the man to come back. After a few seconds with no supervision, I would have eaten the first marshmallow. The reason I know I would have failed that test is because I have failed so many real-life tests just like it.

I am so glad that my early bent toward failure was not the end of the story. So many of the challenges I have faced in life have been about learning to overcome my natural leaning toward failure. Ultimately, that's all these tendencies were: tendencies that I was able to overcome through personal and professional growth.

If you have a bent toward failure too, it's not the end of the story for you either. You can overcome. This book will help you get there.

Confession 3: I am not there yet.

As an author, speaker, business coach, and trainer, I have worked with thousands of people who are living below their potential. I have seen the transformation of many of these people as they are released to live goal-oriented, deliberate, and more fulfilled lives after listening to my speeches and participating in my workshops and coaching sessions. But, as successful as I've been, I know I still have a long way to go toward maximizing my potential. So, I have two coaches and several mentors myself, and I continue to learn at an aggressive pace.

The Place Called "There"

Of all the creatures on earth, human beings are the only ones that can set their own course. I admit, we are partly instinctual and driven to survive like all other creatures in the animal kingdom, but we are unique in our capacity to choose our thoughts, emotions, and actions, and it is that uniqueness that gives us the power to dream of our lives being greater, to determine how we will live, and, ultimately, to establish where and how we'll finish life. The shame is that most of us will follow our instinctive nature and succumb to the power of rejection, the fear of the unknown, and, worst of all, the fear of what we could become should we embrace the fullness of our true nature. The good news, as I said, is that it doesn't have to be that way.

What would happen if you decided you could be great at what you do and passionate about why you are doing it? What would happen if you left an impact so large during your short time on this planet that it would be talked about for ages to come? I can assure you that if you truly decided to, you would almost certainly attain that. As British Prime Minister Benjamin Disraeli said, "Nothing can resist the human will that will stake even its existence on its stated purpose."[6]

The Pitfalls of Self-Improvement Literature

Truthfully, we must allow ourselves to become the type of people who command the results we want in life. As James Allen, a pioneer of the self-help movement, wrote, "Men do not attract that which they want, but that which they are."[7] Yet too many people are waiting for something mystical to take place rather than initiating the change that is required to reap success.

Much ink has been spilled over trying to discover the keys to commanding from life that which we want. Even so, I feel there is a gap in self-improvement literature—a gap that I found myself in. I became lost in these books, trying to follow the suggestions explicitly. No matter how much I read or studied, or how much effort I put into behavioral and personality adjustments, I found myself falling short.

I erroneously concluded that the vast majority of people who fall short of the achievements they desire, like I did in the past, just lack micro-steps that will catapult them into achieving their dreams. We need micro-steps, I thought, to empower us. But I wondered what those micro-steps were. To find them, I looked in the biographies of successful people.

The Pitfalls of Biographies of Successful People

Astrophysicist and author Neil deGrasse Tyson suggests that wisdom is the ability to look at patterns in life and connect the dots.[8] After all I have seen in twenty years in business coaching, that definition resonated with me. I asked, "Is there a pattern to commanding from life all that we want—or is it a pattern that is fit for some, but not for all?"

Some people, those who are wise, will look at life's normal cycles and events, see the patterns, and learn from them. They'll learn to anticipate what's going to happen next and be able to change their behavior to grasp success, where before they held failure.

But what about me, an average student? Obtaining that kind of wisdom isn't rocket science, but it does require us to observe and reflect on the affairs and events of life in order to discover how we should act to get the results we desire.

After reading biographies of such figures as Abraham Lincoln, W. E. B. Du Bois, and Martin Luther King Jr., I came to the conclusion that many people become successful by accident. What I mean by this is that they become successful through no intentional effort of their own. Success seems to come naturally to them. At the same time, successful people, such as historical leaders, exhibit widely varying personalities and behaviors. Yet no one can deny that this wide range of leaders has indeed achieved high levels of success.

Unfortunately, the experts who investigate the lives of great men and women and who articulate the mysteries behind their success often don't say enough. Their books, written about the people who made a difference, are typically historically accurate, but if viewed as success literature, they're largely incomplete. I concluded that it is difficult to derive success action steps from the books written about historical figures.

This is not to say that I don't appreciate the biographies that describe and explain the lives of successful people. Had it not been for many of these books, which I plumbed for self-improvement tips, I would not have developed as much as I have. I believe, however, that many of the lessons put forth in these books are not sufficiently explained or are so vague that I could not easily apply them.

For instance, one best-selling author did research on Lee Iacocca and told of how he was a great and selfless leader.[9] But before the ink was dry, another author wrote a book pointing out how ridiculously selfish Iacocca was.[10] He used Iacocca's story to show why his leadership was limited and short-lived. And again, while one best-selling author idolized Henry Ford as the model of the successful industrialist,[11] another best-selling author used him as an example of a disempowering leader.[12]

Another tragedy is that I often find leadership development books, many of which incorporate biographical information about successful people, to be more about ideas for the already highly skilled. Reading these books achieved the result of making me think about the things I needed to do to become more successful. However, that which actually makes for success is what we do when we are not thinking. It is our unconscious habits that determine our success. So, the biographies of successful people didn't go far enough for me.

Successful People Themselves

Many successful people are those who, through intuition, did the right thing, at the right time, while responding to the right opportunity. Whether scientists like Newton, Edison, or Carver or politicians like Lincoln, Kennedy, or Reagan, many successful people simply did the right things at the right time because they instinctively understood the secrets to success. Unfortunately, I have found that very few people who understand something instinctively also know it in a way that enables them to teach it.

As a case in point, take Ted Williams, a Major League Baseball player. He claims the all-time batting average rank of seventh and was asked to become a batting coach after he retired from playing baseball in 1960. The assumption was that he was so talented that he would be a great asset to any ball club as a trainer. The challenge arose when he would give batters instruction from his perspective, and players with less ability weren't able to capture his vision and presence of mind. His instruction was worthless.[13]

Many top figures have gained success through discipline or by acting almost unconsciously according to a well-designed script. They attribute their victories to hard work, intense dedication, or never losing faith. However, there are many people who work hard and dream big, never give up, and still never achieve what they are after, so that's not the whole story.

Here's another angle. Many successful people were brought up in adversity. That adversity gave them unwavering resolve not to be victimized again, and they used this energy and power to succeed. In many cases, contemporary research suggests that their resolve was created before they achieved cognitive awareness, usually before the age of six.

Other successful people inherited success by being developed in a positive atmosphere where their self-esteem was nurtured. This allowed them to face life with a never-give-up attitude. Positive events somehow groomed them for success. This, also, is socialized strength that shapes children before cognitive awareness.

The influences that shape accomplished people are many: intuition, discipline, hardships that developed successful survivors, or loving parents who instilled a sense of confidence and self-worth in their children. However, they are shaped, I find that most high achievers consistently have a certain drive and inner strength that allow them to overcome what most people cannot.

Did These Examples Help Me?

The problem with all these reasons for success is that they didn't help someone like me: a person who fought fearlessly for many years for success without ever finding it. I had trouble gaining control over the three areas I see as necessary for success: the inner realm, the social realm, and the power realm.

These three realms must be conquered in order to succeed. We must gain the confidence to face who we are (in our inner realm), to behave how we need to behave (finding peace within our social realm), and to design the impact we want to have (in our power realm).

We need confidence to face our inner realm, to change our default programming. We need courage to interact within our social realm, to cultivate successful social habits. We need consistency to create our power realm, to repeat right thought patterns and behaviors over time to reap rewards.

In the brilliant book *Influencer*, Kerry Patterson identifies that if you want to change results, you must first identify what behaviors you need to give you the desired results.[14] In contrast, in conversation, many people exhaust the topic of what we should stop doing. Leaving it at that, they don't go far enough to figure out what they should be doing instead because they also don't start at the beginning by looking at their thought patterns.

Some self-help gurus look for the outcomes they want, and then they package and repackage outcomes as desired principles or laws in their books. Those of us who are less intuitive bang our heads on the proverbial wall trying to behave outcomes. The sad truth is that you cannot behave an outcome. Also, the outcome one person wants may not be what another person wants, so a book about outcomes as principles is useful to very few people.

So, I'm sorry to say that the hundreds of books I read searching for the clues to success ultimately left me only a little further ahead and not where I wanted to be.

Life as a Cycle of Events to Understand

There are two letters in the English language that almost make a word. "Re" is a grammatical construct that symbolizes an action that occurs again or anew. It is fitting to have such a symbol in the language since it supports the idea of life as a cycle of events that we must repeat until we get it right.

Some people never attain success in life because they reject life's lessons from their cycle of events. They remain unaware that the reason for life's events is to teach us. For example, when things go wrong and we don't learn from them, life often gives us a second chance. In the words of philosopher George Santayana, "Those who cannot remember the past are condemned to repeat it."[15]

To be successful in life, we must become students of it. It is commonly said that experience is the greatest teacher, yet only a fool would choose to learn everything through personal experience. The experiences of others often teach us enough to be successful in life. If we pay attention, we'll see patterns in the lives of those who have gone before us and in the lives of our contemporaries. Studying these patterns and applying the wisdom learned from them is often sufficient action to excel in any endeavor.

Discipline, however, is required to study and to act on our newly acquired wisdom. Acting consistently will propel us forward, people will notice our growth, and this will open to us new paths for opportunity. Throughout life, we receive open doors to advance, closed doors to stop, timely doors that say "wait," and forks in the road to choose. The choices we make are defined by our character. Preparedness gives us the power to make additional right choices.

This book is meant to be a tool that will assist in preparing those who desire to succeed but feel that they have somehow lacked opportunity. Each chapter will explore a thought pattern by giving you concepts, occasional action steps, and with additional review and reflection questions in the companion workbook to help you think about and possibly adjust your thought patterns.

If you desire to build your physical body, you need a vision of what you want to look and feel like, an awareness of what it will take you to get there, and a system that will break the challenge down into manageable daily actions. You must also start by developing muscles where they cannot be seen before they will impact what can be seen. The core muscles underneath need to form before they begin to show outwardly. Similarly, if you want to become a success, you must have a picture of what success means to you, an awareness of what it will take to become this future you, and a thought system that will make the journey manageable. This book details a thought system to base your success on.

Early congratulations on taking a step toward personal and professional success.

—Dr. Stephen J. Crawford

CHAPTER 1

REBOOT

/rē'bo͞ ot/

You cannot separate your identity from your perspective.
All that you are and every experience you've had
color how you see things. It is your lens.
—John C. Maxwell[1]

I'll never forget the moment I won my first trophy. I was called up in front of the entire school for having the best attitude in my first-grade class. I kept the trophies well into my midtwenties. When children know they are special, this frames how they will engage with the world. It may not surprise you to hear that most people in their early childhood years are superstars in their own eyes. Adults usually treat children from birth to early adolescence with adoration and pleasantness, affirmation and congratulations, making the children feel like superstars. Do you remember that in your own life?

Even if we weren't celebrated, our perspective only allowed us to see ourselves as the center of the universe. No one sees life objectively;

we see it through a lens that begins to form before we are even born. We may begin life by seeing through a lens of adult comments such as "You can't do that," or "You'll never be able to." Trust me, I heard those comments later in life, but my beginning was a different story—I started life believing I was a superstar! Early on, my parents, grandparents, and church community instilled that feeling in me.

My mother, an educator, offered me an incredible childhood development. She took her time to train me to read by the time I entered preschool. By kindergarten, the school offered to move me up a grade, but my parents refused to move me beyond my age group.

My mother insisted on asking thought-provoking questions to us children at a very young age. Because of that, I also mastered the art of critical thinking and communication skills before many children in my preschool class. Before I turned four years old, my father thought I should become an attorney because of the way I craftily presented my cases to avoid punishment. In my early years, he felt it was reasonable to allow me to understand why I was being punished. After I learned to talk myself out of a few too many spankings, he decided it was just as well if I didn't understand.

I respected my father and grandfather immensely when I was growing up. Actually, I idolized my grandfather. He was a powerful communicator, a pastor, and a community activist. As I watched my grandfather lead people, I decided I wanted to do what he did. I didn't understand leadership or influence, but I knew I wanted what he wielded. When I was five, I told him, "I want to preach." He beamed with pride and told me about the seriousness and importance of that role. From that day forward, I felt he began to give me preferential treatment, and I was a standout among his grandchildren. He announced my intentions to the church, and the congregation gave me an overflow of affirmation, congratulations, and appreciation from that time on.

Church members praised me for my courage to engage with adults and my attentiveness to the lessons being taught. Schoolteachers also encouraged and praised me for my congeniality, behavior, and academics. It was a little difficult to get praise at home from siblings (I'm the fifth of nine), but my parents praised me enough to persuade me to always pursue excellence.

In my early years, I was surrounded by people who praised my abilities to perform on cue and communicate in ways that were persuasive. Thus, my identity was formed—I saw myself as a successful, persuasive communicator. Now I realize there may be variations, but many people have stories like mine.

The quality of your lens will determine the quality of your life.

In John Maxwell's *Winning with People*, he speaks of the "Lens Principle," which indicates that we think we see the world, people, and our environment the way they are when, in fact, we see them as we are.[3]

If we have a lens built by strong love and affection, deep empathy, and compassion for others—if we have a great self-image—we will interpret the world in a positive way. We will grow up to be connected to our world in a way that continues to support our growth and development, and we will almost walk our way into a successful, meaningful life. If, however, we experience rejection from family and develop a "kill or be killed" mentality and a low self-image, we will struggle all our lives.

Where You Start Matters

Many people erroneously believe that a person's stature in life is a result of some sort of personal endowment that comes due to the worthiness of the individual, the goodness of their character, or the quality of their family. They don't realize how much the person's community makes a difference too. For example, a neighborhood full of the sounds of gunshots and sirens affects an infant's mind much differently than a quiet neighborhood full of children playing.

The state of the child's brain contributes greatly to the formation of self-perception. According to microbiologist Dr. Bruce Lipton, the brain of a child between the ages of two and four operates at the lowest EEG (electroencephalogram) frequency and produces delta waves. The delta state is a state of *hyperlearning* in which children are essentially limitless. They can learn up to five languages and four instruments without any signs of mental fatigue. When children are learning, they are not just translating; they are imprinting an original interpretation of language—and all the nuances that go with it.[4]

The body at that age is processing how to walk—and how to move in the most energy-conserving ways. The child's brain is memorizing words, intonations, sarcasm, and nonverbal expressions that give the words meaning. This rapid rate of learning is one of the miracles of life. When a child swears in public for the first time, parents look embarrassed as if they have no idea how their child heard the word. The parents' look would have persuaded us to believe that they had no part in the child's swearing had the child not used the word in such a remarkably accurate context.

A child between the ages of four and six spends a significant amount of time in the delta phase, but more of their brain activity advances into the theta phase, whether awake or sleeping.[5] The study of theta brain waves in children is not as advanced as in adults, so we'll look at the theta phase in adults next. It is common for adults to spend time in the theta phase between sleeping and waking or under a hypnotic state. Scientists often refer to this as the *twilight reverie* state. As adults, we often experience this state when our minds are caught between dream and reality.[6]

No child comes out of the womb walking and talking, and they do not attend classes to learn. A child begins with learning through observation; then they try and fail their way to walking, talking, eating, and thousands of other far more complex actions. They accomplish these things invariably because, in the early stages of life, we lack self-judgment and criticism, which tend to cripple us later in life. At that young age, we don't have an interpretation of what failing is.

So, we learn to talk, beginning with sounds, and they become words, and then sentences and paragraphs, all the way to full-blown dissertations. For walking, we begin with struggling, then movements, then crawling, stumbling, and walking, and then we can run. But if a child were restricted by the fear that they might never fully talk, or by the fear that they would never fully walk or run, they would begin to question their own abilities. It is said that if a child were born with the self-consciousness of an adult, they wouldn't be able to walk until age seventy, if at all.[7]

From the age of six and up, as the child spends more and more time in the alpha phase, self-consciousness begins to grow. The alpha phase is recorded by EEGs when a patient is in a relaxed mental state with their eyes closed.[8] The alpha phase is when we transition from absorbing information to beginning to filter and evaluate it. This means that at six, for the most part, the cup for learning has been shaped, and our character has essentially been formed. This is why it is rumored that the Jesuits would say, "Give me a child until they are six, and I will give you the man." This progression that develops self-consciousness comes with benefits but also at a cost. The benefit is that a person begins to care about what other people think and thus conforms to certain social graces that help us maintain order. The cost is that a person begins to care about what people think, which often leaves us backing down from our goals based on how others might see us.

In contrast, the lack of self-consciousness is what we need if we're going to be successful. We have to be able to approach a goal with a childlike mindset where we're thinking through our struggles and failures—not with judgment, restriction, or resistance but with the image of success ever in our minds.

We have to treat the process as just that—a process. As we're going through it, it brings us closer to our goal, and we're actually learning, step-by-step, what the process looks like. That's the power of embracing childlike thinking: we develop the habits of pressing through failure since it is a natural part of learning.

During the early years, humans can download information faster than at any other time in life. Their preponderance of time in the theta phase is why a child can learn three languages and multiple instruments at the same time without a problem. Children do not have the burden of over processing information. Their fantasy and reality run seamlessly together. This allows them to expand their imagination and experience growth in any area they want to.

It is in the theta phase, in this dreamlike state, that the framing for life and reality begins to take shape.[9] This framing causes either the automatic success mechanism or automatic failure mechanism (as termed by Dr. Maxwell Maltz, who wrote *The New Psycho-Cybernetics*) to take root.[10] We typically download the behaviors, beliefs, and attitudes we observe in our parents, which then become hardwired as synaptic pathways in our subconscious minds.[11] Once programmed, we don't control the program, and we aren't able to consciously process this worldview. Our worldview creates a map that orients us to our borders, our limitations, and our directions.

It is estimated that we experience, on average, sixty thousand thoughts per day. It is also estimated that fifty thousand of them are negative. The amazing part is that 90 percent of these thoughts don't change from day to day. These patterns of automatic thought are often the only difference between one human and another, according to David Rock in his book *Quiet Leadership*.[12] This is why one retail shop in Benton, Arkansas, went out of business while another just two blocks away became the largest retailer in the world. It's the reason Dick and Maurice McDonald launched ten franchises and all failed, but Ray Kroc built McDonald's into the largest franchise in the world. Same industry, same opportunity, only the thinking of the leader was different.

Our thinking shapes our lens; therefore, perception is reality to the one who believes it. This thinking goes down to the cellular level, and the study of it has formed a science called *epigenetics*. Epigenetic research has discovered the mechanism by which genes interpret their environment. Epigenetics is the engineer that interprets the blueprint. Those who have the appetite to review Bruce Lipton's book *The Biology of Belief* will be amazed at how shifting a perception can reorganize one's biology to reinforce an existing belief.[13] There are many reasons why it's difficult to change our lens once it has formed—add our biology to the mix.

The cell has two functions as it relates to stimuli in the environment: first, growth and a response toward stimuli, and second, protection and a response away from stimuli. Along those lines, the body is a reflection of the mind. If the body considers something a threat, it shuts down blood from flowing to the forebrain and protects the body as it prepares for battle. Similarly, when fear is triggered, the mind shuts down the emotions, the nervous system, and blood flow. In the opposite way, love opens up our blood flow, emotions, and minds to more possibilities.[14] Experiencing personal growth requires a loving mindset toward ourselves.

We will now approach the amazing miracle of brain development through the lens of sociology. When we are about six years old, when the brain is operating in an alpha state, critical, concrete thinking begins.[15] As humans, we begin to associate meaning to our importance in relation to others. The most powerful influence in this developmental behavior is the one that impacts our self-image. We create a picture of the people, institutions, and systems around us, and we attribute meaning to each. The most significant meaning we create is the view we have of ourselves. This is what makes the family unit so powerful when it comes to shaping a child's self-perception, and thereby that child's future.

I mentioned before that most people are superstars in their own eyes during early childhood. The element of competition has not yet completely settled in, and most children can just have fun living in their own world.

You Cannot Win the Comparison Game

In adolescence, people usually engage in activities that play to their strengths, and this leaves some feeling pretty good about themselves and others feeling inadequate. There tends to be a humbling experience called failure that awakens people to their humanity. I was no stranger to this experience.

As a child, I was highly commended for my bravery in public speaking, my skill and zeal for memorization, and my passion for demonstrating leadership among my peers. Until the fourth grade, I don't remember a single award ceremony in which I wasn't the recipient, be it academic, leadership, athletic, or otherwise.

I was on top of the world. When I watched a cartoon or movie, I thought the superheroes in stories always pointed back to me. I was Underdog, Superman, Batman, and the Incredible Hulk. I thought I could do anything. I felt there was nothing out of my grasp. I had a healthy self-image and an understanding that if I was rejected, it was only by a poor soul who didn't understand who I was. I was a great salesman in the making. After a while, I expected to win at everything—until I didn't.

At some point in my childhood, I stopped winning every race, every spelling bee, and every PTO sales competition. At that point, adults no longer stopped to tell me how cute I was. I have to admit I didn't miss them pinching my cheeks, but I could feel that something was missing. When other people's names were called to receive the prizes that I had worked for, I felt somehow crippled or defective, like my best was not good enough anymore.

It may seem that I am being overly dramatic about the experience of failure, and maybe I am. But before I concede to this, you have to question for a moment why, if everyone is created so gifted and so gloriously different from each other, so many respond the same way to failure. It's kind of crazy because compared to a frog, I can sing really well, but after my superstar status wore off, I was only comparing my voice to the best singer in the choir. It's as if I became obsessed with looking for the things in which I suffered from an inferior skill or talent rather than being obsessed with what I could excel and grow in.

Marcus Buckingham looks at this mindset in his book *StandOut*. He says we become obsessed with what we aren't good at, with our weaknesses. We refuse to look at the areas in which we're supposed to be incredibly brilliant.[16]

This deficiency focus left me discouraged and hopeless. I suppose my thinking was that if I wasn't the best in everything, I must be average. My conclusion was that I should reduce my effort and stop trying. I was lulled to the level of those other poor souls I had previously pitied.

Why is humanity plagued with complacency and overwhelmed with mediocrity? As Earl Nightingale would put it, "We conform."[17] Humans have the power of will, emotion, intelligence, memory, intuition, and imagination, yet even with such a complex skill set, the majority of us spend our lives without ever tapping into the potential that could make us great.

Let's look at what it means to not be great. No amount of luck can transform a person with a horrible attitude into a success because they'll be too busy complaining to see the opportunities right in front of them. In addition, a person who experienced luck once, such as in winning the lottery, is not called a success because success is more than just a temporary event or situation.

Also, no one looks at a bitter old man, no matter how rich he is, and says they want to be like him. To be a "success" is not defined by having skill in one area and being broken and damaged in many other areas at the same time.

On the contrary, people look at individuals who are satisfied in every area and consider them successful. Success is a combination of a person's wins, personality, and relationships. It involves pursuing a continuous line of improvement. But how does a person realize a continuous line of improvement?

A Hero's Response to Failure

What separates successful people from unsuccessful ones is how they respond to failure. History holds up many heroes who were never well off financially and who failed many times. Heroes such as Abraham Lincoln, Phillis Wheatley, Thomas Edison, and Harriet Tubman suffered through many trials and failures, but it was how they continued on despite rejection that caused them to mark American history forever.

For example, Abraham Lincoln's list of failures between 1832 and 1858 is eleven items long, according to Abraham Lincoln Online.[18] Nevertheless, he was elected president in 1860. Phillis Wheatley, an African American slave known as one of the greatest poets of the eighteenth century, could not find a publisher for her poems in the American colonies.[19] Thomas Edison lost all the money and years of time he invested in trying to find an economical way to mine iron ore.[20] When Harriet Tubman fled from the slave state of Maryland to the free state of Pennsylvania, her husband did not go with her. Her marriage failed, and her husband eventually remarried.[21]

All of these successful Americans experienced failure, but failure did not define them. Have you experienced failure? If so, it does not have to define you either.

Gain Strength from Failure

Many self-improvement books teach us how to succeed, but few teach us how to fail. John Maxwell tackled this topic by penning the book *Failing Forward*, in which he teaches that the seed of success lies in each failed attempt.[22] If I had learned this earlier in life, it might have reshaped my thinking enough to affect my foundations.

Failure, for most people, causes them to become average, their motivation to dwindle, and their attitude to be one of disappointment.

If they don't change and pick up the pieces of shattered success, their strengths begin to atrophy.

My story is far too common; the same experiences of failure that confronted me are similar to experiences that make many people feel average. What makes people feel like failures in life (and by a failure, I mean a person who is unable to set and accomplish their desired goals) is their inability to bounce back from failure. When failure becomes internalized and a person cannot separate their action from their character, they become a failure. Many, like me in my youth, have not developed the emotional fortitude to overcome rejection. Failure diminishes our ability to return to the task with enthusiasm. Failure injures us all. It hurts our pride, wounds our egos, and challenges our self-esteem.

However, there is a great difference between playing injured and playing crippled. To be injured means that you're in a healing process by which you will eventually recover. To be crippled means that you have been set back permanently. Injury may be physical or emotional; to be crippled is to be unable to move due to injury. We all have been injured, but we must choose whether we will allow the injury to cripple us.

Action Step

Think about a time when you have been injured. Did you recover completely, partially, or not at all? How does that injury affect you now?

You Matter

Humans invent in response to need:

- The need for light at night encouraged the creation of the light bulb.

- The need for faster transportation led to the development of planes, trains, and automobiles.
- The need for communication inspired email and cell phones.

We start with needs; we are creative beings that invent solutions. In the same way, would not the Designer of the entire universe have created us in response to some type of need or purpose, along with a plan?

I believe every person has a purpose to which their life is called—and that the miracle of you is not an accident. I believe the Designer had a purpose and a plan for you before He created you.

Michael Behe, professor of microbiology at Lehigh University, describes life in his book *Darwin's Black Box* as too unimaginably complex for anything to have happened by accident.[23] It follows that everything about you is intentional. Your soul has an internal hard-wiring that yearns for significance. I believe God placed that inside you so you would see your life as an adventure of passionate discovery instead of a series of failures.

Rejection Shapes Us

According to the philosopher Dallas Willard, rejection is the most powerful human impulse.[24] In his book *Renovation of the Heart*, he suggests that our hearts (the center of our lives) are shaped by three things: rejection, acceptance, and our response to both.

Take, for example, the former practice of training elephants to be circus animals. Natural conditioning was used. A baby elephant was placed in a leg brace that restricted them from breaking loose. As any wild animal would, they spent a lot of time trying to break free from the chain, but they did not have the necessary strength.

When the circus elephants became fully grown animals of amazing strength, they would only have had to snap the chain around their ankle, and they could run free. However, they had been conditioned by childhood experiences that limited their ability to truly be themselves. Daily they repeated the course that had been set before them because their past failures crippled their strength by crippling their perception.[25]

As humans, we have been conditioned as well. We have been crippled by failure, and our failures have convinced us to give up on our dreams. Pain has stunted our growth, preventing us from going forward—even when going forward is the right thing to do. We need to penetrate through to our carefully protected psyches. We will benefit from harnessing our psyches to develop the "good thought habits" we need to fulfill our dreams.

To develop good thought habits, we must return to childlike thinking. We must exercise our thought habit "muscles" over and over again, through failure, to reach beneficial thought habits.

The eight thought habits I suggest in this book are not so vague that you won't know how to practice them, so aloof that they seem unattainable, or so difficult that you may not possess the skills to perform them. The thought habits in this book are simple enough to grasp, but they are challenging enough to make a difference in your life.

The Power to Change

Resilience is the ability to bounce back from failure with the same amount of enthusiasm, belief, and energy you had when you first tried. When a person is truly resilient, almost immediately after failure, they begin to look over the data of the failed attempt. They can do this because they are not surprised by failure; they accept it as a natural part of the process. After failure, they actually begin to see options.

In *Developing the Leader within You* John Maxwell says, "Problems can stop you temporarily. You are the only one who can stop you permanently."[26] If there is a situation you cannot do something about, it is not a problem; it is a fact of life, and you learn what to do to work with it. Resilient people are able to determine the difference between problems and facts of life. Though problems may affect their stride, problems will in no way diminish their progress.

For many of us, when the fabric of our confidence is diminished and our attempts to be successful fail, further attempts are made with less enthusiasm, less spirit, and perhaps a bit of bitterness and skepticism. The bottom line is that even if we continue to try, meeting failure after failure, our attempts will be inadequate. The only way we could possibly succeed is by a stroke of luck.

However, when a person is resilient, they approach every challenge just like they did the first time. They are not worn down by failure because they know that their diligence and tenacious determination will eventually pay off. This book is meant to inspire you to take the leap into trying multiple times to succeed with enthusiasm—as if failure were impossible.

What will your legacy be? Do you have what it takes to be a success in your field, the courage to fulfill your dream, and the ability to determine your future? In every great leader's story, there is a thread of unwavering resilience that allows them to face challenges and overcome them. When they achieved their goal, they were called successful. The same can be true for you!

Between the reality and the dream, there are many negative forces that will come against you. These negative forces will challenge your beliefs, detour your vision, and question your ethics. Before you achieve success, there will be resistance that may cause others to turn around, but with the thought habits you'll learn in this book, you will gain the mental and emotional fortitude to continue your journey to success.

CHAPTER 2

REFRAME

/rēˈfrām/

Disappointment is the nurse of wisdom.
—Sir Boyle Roche

I was devastated! No, I was outraged! I felt cheated out of obtaining a position that I felt I deserved. I was ready to quit City Leaders Nonprofit (real organization, but fictional name), which had just turned me down for a promotion because I felt they had no right to give the position to someone else. I left the coffee shop angry and agitated, and I resolved I wouldn't allow this to happen again.

I had just met with one of City Leaders' board members, who used the famous words, "We've decided to go in a different direction." I had been rejected for a second time from a job that would allow me to fully work in my sweet spot. In addition to my full-time job, I had already been committing more than forty hours a week to this job that paid me for less than twenty hours a week.

It was clear to me that no one loved this organization more than

I did, especially the board of directors, who only participated in our annual meetings and a quarterly board meeting now and then. To explain why I was so distraught about this particular rejection, let me give a little more context.

The First Time They Said No

When I was originally hired, I worked diligently, far beyond my job description, to see City Leaders succeed. I had found something I truly believed in with all my heart. I spent years observing the problems within City Leaders and months discussing with colleagues how we might improve the nonprofit.

Those six years at that job were extraordinary for using the best of my gifts and abilities. You know one of those jobs that allows you to work in your sweet spot? J. Robert Clinton uses the term "convergence" in his book *The Making of a Leader* to describe the goal of one's life. Convergence is when a leader is working in an environment where 80 percent of their gifting matches with 80 percent of their responsibilities.[1] In my first professional job, this nonprofit job, I had the privilege of working in the direction of convergence of 40–50 percent of my life gifts, passion, and values.

Nothing could be better than this, I thought. But then the president decided to step down, and an opening emerged at the top spot of City Leaders, which I loved and wanted to commit my life to. I felt it was a marriage made in heaven—me and the position I coveted.

I was told in no uncertain terms by the previous president that he would recommend me to the board since I was his right-hand man during his tenure. His confidence in me was based on how seriously I believed in the organization's mission and the fact that I was responsible for most of the innovation within City Leaders. I also had an assistant whose organizational skills complemented my visionary leadership style. She and I spoke about the possibilities and were confident that we would get called to lead the organization and do things that had never been done in our industry.

So, imagine our surprise when the board of directors hired for the position a high-profile leader who had a good reputation and political connections. We felt let down that I did not receive the position, but we hoped for the best from our new leaders.

Our new leader was allowed to keep his full-time political job in hopes that he would use his influence to support City Leaders. Unfortunately for the organization, he only gave his reputation to the nonprofit. He did not advance our mission by reaching out to his connections or spending more than a cursory amount of time leading us. It became clear years later when we found that people in his organization didn't know that he was even filling the role.

I felt robbed, betrayed, and misled. These negative feelings were not aimed at people; instead, they swirled around the idea that I was inadequate. This was not an isolated thought, but a remembering that validated a thought I had lived with for a long time. I used the opportunity to leave the organization at that time and study abroad. I went to Costa Rica to study Spanish and spent the entire year stunned, but still dreaming that I could return and secure the top spot in City Leaders.

The frustration was that, after I returned to the United States, other jobs in my field were rare. I couldn't find one. I sought a job in my field for well over a month before I resigned myself to taking whatever I could get. I ended up taking a job selling cars. In the interview, the hiring manager asked me why a guy with a master's degree and in the second year of a doctoral program would want to sell cars. I was honest; I replied, "For now, I just need a job."

Well, I didn't need to read Patrick Lencioni's book *The Three Signs of a Miserable Job* to recognize what misery looks like. As a matter of fact, I could have given Lencioni anecdotes. The pain of going to work every day was unbelievable. Daily, I walked into an atmosphere where the goal was to get people who knew little about a particular vehicle to pay more than market value for it. That violated my conscience. That was not success in my eyes. Even worse, I recognized that many of the successful people I knew didn't follow all the rules that I did. I was told that education and hard work was the way. Instead, I was a second-year doctoral student who worked tirelessly at every job I ever held—and I was stuck.

I hated going to a place where the management team showed little leadership. The management team was filled with excellent managers who knew how to make a profit, but they knew little about leadership. I wanted to be in an environment that would challenge me to grow.

There is nothing more frustrating for me than a J-O-B. The word *job* speaks of everything that is wrong with how we live. It's a cold word that tells you when to clock in and when to clock out. Who has an emotional attachment to a job? Not me. I wanted to be in a position that aligned with my passion. The word *vocation* actually stems from the Latin word associated with a calling. A vocation is more exciting than a job because it allows us to pursue work for which we have been called.

I was miserable. While none of my colleagues ever took breaks in fear they would lose a sale, I decided to escape during my lunch hour and go to Barnes & Noble to read—and it was there that I began thinking of the ideas that became this book. I began writing this sixteen years ago because I wanted to know why so many people find themselves stuck. My unique gift is to identify patterns, so I've been able to distill all I've learned into the pages that follow. I want to speak to those who, like me, refuse to die in a dealership when we are called to set others ablaze. Now, some people are called to sell cars, and there is dignity in whatever a person may feel called to do, but this is written for those who feel trapped and see no exit doors when they know deep inside that they are meant to work and live at a higher level.

I decided I wanted convergence, but I would settle for doing something that fulfilled me at least 20 percent. I was willing to settle for anything that, at minimum, used my gifts. All I really wanted was to find a position I was good at and into which I could put all my strength. I wanted to use all of my abilities and begin to explore the potential that I believe was put in me at birth.

Three questions arose:

- Would I ever become the man I desired to be?
- Could I ever accomplish the dreams that lay deep in my heart?
- How long would it be before I could do what I loved?

There was only one answer, and it was buried deep beneath all the pain and rejection. The answer was a resounding *yes* to hope! I knew that it was only a matter of time before my dreams would be fulfilled.

I believed if I focused and trusted the process, the dreams that were mere fantasies would eventually begin to yield fruit greater than anything I could imagine. In one of my darkest moments of doubt, that revelation came to me.

In the midst of that dark time of feeling lost and without hope, my previous organization's president invited me back to my previous position. Then our new fearless leader abandoned his post. He showed up for less than half the board meetings. During his tenure, he missed all but two weekly scheduled staff meetings (he made the first two).

Needless to say, under his leadership, the program lost its potency. At its peak, the program worked as a collaborative effort with more than one hundred organizations and effectively trained about three hundred leaders a year. In less than two years, under the new president's leadership, those numbers fell to eleven leaders trained with only four partner organizations.

The board contemplated shutting down, but I addressed them and convinced them I could reenergize the organization. However, by that time, the organization had developed such a bad reputation with its constituency that very few people were willing to talk about it.

I forged ahead, interviewing anyone who would take my call, and received honest responses and candid feedback about what former partners thought it would take to reshape City Leaders. In the process, we created strategic alliances between our training company and organizations that were willing to partner with us who could help reduce overhead. This was important because the board was close to declaring a shutdown.

I worked tirelessly to redevelop the organization's mission, vision, values, and direction, and I got buy-ins from influential leaders in the community. We knew these buy-ins would prove critical to the success of our organization. Then something surprising happened. We applied for and received a grant that would prove to be the validation we needed to convince the board to move forward. Immediately, the board decided to hire a new president. Due to my devotion and skill, I believed the board would finally hire me for that role.

I was confident that the interview was merely a formality. I began making plans to restore the former glory of the organization. Then, a week later, the board told me that they valued me and appreciated what my assistant and I had accomplished, but they wanted a different skill set at the top.

After working relentlessly with a team of strong leaders who pulled this organization from the brink of collapse to being ready to move into the next phase of our mission, our reward was for the board to hand the reins to an outsider who knew nothing about the price we paid and, therefore, could not appreciate the urgency of the mandate we were under to make this work.

The board of directors was under the impression that the downfall of the previous leader occurred because his life was so demanding. The board's new idea was to bring someone out of retirement who had nothing but time and who had led other organizations like this before. She would put our organization back on the map, the board thought.

I spent the next two years of my life watching the resources of City Leaders squandered, paying someone who acknowledged upon her exit that she never quite understood the heart of what it was we did. After she resigned, the board finally made me president of the organization.

The point of this long story is that I reached my goal despite many setbacks. I did not know what the end of the story would be when I started, but I had an outcome I wanted. I could have resigned to go look for a position that was easier to obtain any number of times. But deep inside, I had a passion, not so much for personal achievement, but for the success of the organization. This perspective drove me to rebound every time I didn't reach my goal. I continued to use my gifts to contribute toward this organization that was making a difference.

If you meet me, you'll see that I am a dreamer. I'll be the first to admit that my gift of dreaming big dreams leaves me disappointed more often than not. However, my ability to see things in unconventional ways that provide solutions previously unthought-of of also gives me an edge. Along those lines, I continue to find improvements and write them down, search for root causes, and find even greater solutions to problems I come across. By the time I am done with a project, everyone who is a part of it knows that this is what makes me tick.

Most of us have been caught in a cycle that prohibits us from chasing our dreams. We have chosen to follow in the footsteps of so many in our industrialized society while the dreamer inside of us dies. We work to pursue wealth and comfort and live to provide material goods while the most passionate part of us accepts the status quo. I believe that deep inside every one of us is a dream, but somewhere along the way, we are told to stop dreaming and find a job.

The part of us that dreams has the ability to create things that don't yet exist; it is important not to abandon this part of our personalities. It is critical that we don't allow the dreamer part of us to die. We have to learn at some point to stand up and shout with a loud voice, "I refuse to let my dreams die! I refuse to just find another job!

I will pursue my dreams to the best of my abilities!" Pursuing our dreams allows us to be much more than average or normal.

Failure is a necessary part of success, so we cannot be afraid to fail. Despite everything I had been through—all my failed attempts and all the rejections I experienced—the ability to dream again arose within me.

I want to share what I discovered along the way about failure and success, so I am writing this book. I've designed it to be simple to interpret for all those who, like me, are tired of excuses and exhausted by the success flavor of the month.

There are too many power seminars and get-rich schemes that flicker with activity but lack actual results. I have seen the broken-heartedness and the crying eyes of people whose dreams were shattered into pieces. The world is full of jaded people who were only trying to uncover the wisdom of the universe in order to point them to health, wealth, and happiness. You don't have to be one of those people. Keep reading.

Four Lenses

When you're reading a book, it is crucial to observe your context. By that, I mean it is important to be aware of the lenses through which you interpret the content. I want to offer you four lenses for reading this book to magnify your results.

Above and Below the Line

As an executive coach, I work with business leaders every day, and I have found that no matter how good the coaching is, if the participant is fixed on blaming others, making excuses, or denying reality, there is nothing that can be done. Coaching is about awareness and responsibility. The only person who can grow is the one who refuses to release their power to circumstances.

In *The 15 Commitments of Conscious Leadership*, the authors share that they often speak at a conference attended by some of the smartest investment bankers in the world.[2] One of them pulls out their marker and draws a single black line on a whiteboard. They mention that every leader is either above or below this line at any given time.

This line is really a perspective through which we can plan our day or choose our mate. It plays a part in every decision you have ever made and will make in the future. The line informs your attitude and is a foundation for your belief system. The system is binary, not a continuum, meaning you are not somewhat below or somewhat above the line. You are either above the line or below it.

Below the line is where we choose blame, excuses, and denial. We choose to be closed and defensive, which doesn't allow us to see options because our protective nature has been alerted. We choose to be committed to being right. No one else can persuade us against our beliefs because they have become irrefutable in our own thinking.

It is below the line that collaboration ends, creativity dies, animosity brews, and toxicity results. Below the line, there is no winning. Because of the toxic environment, the highest score doesn't mean you won because you are too miserable to celebrate.

The below-the-line person chooses one of three roles: the victim, the villain, or the hero. The victim blames everyone else. A victim believes problems are not their fault and that they have been wronged. The villain takes all the blame on themselves. At first glance, it appears that villains are taking responsibility, but you will see that they are just self-degrading. The tip-off is that the villain does not offer a solution. The hero tries to avoid the conflict and saves the day by denying reality. Heroes restrict the options and are opposed to solving the problem as a team.

A person who is above the line chooses to take responsibility even if it's not their fault. They refuse to believe the solution is out of their control. Above the line, they look for options and remain curious. They know that change is not fatal—but failure to change could be. Above the line, they remain committed to learning, growing, attempting, failing, and bouncing back. They embrace the idea promoted by *How to Say a Few Words*: "Success is going from failure to failure without losing enthusiasm."[3]

Those who choose above-the-line living will experience negative events because that happens to us all. The difference is that those who choose to live above the line do not look for someone to blame, point out whose fault it is, or act as if the problem doesn't exist. They actively look for options and seek creative problem-solving.

The above-the-line person also takes on three roles: the coach, the challenger, and the creator. The coach leads with questions and positions the team in nonjudgmental discovery to search for options. The challenger anticipates that everyone wants to win. They will throw down a challenge they are confident will be accepted, and that allows the team to reach the goal. The creator will explore ideas without denying reality, causing the team to engage at a higher level.

Maybe you have figured out by now that I want you to read this text from above the line. No matter how helpful the principles are in this book, *Too Stupid to Fail*, if you come to the words with judgment, looking to find fault and blame for why you have not achieved more than you have up to this point, you will finish this book with failure and self-judgment. However, if you come to the text looking for options you haven't seen, you will grow beyond where you have been.

Checkpoints versus Road Maps

Make no mistake about it, a road map is a great thing when you need to get to a very specific destination at a specific time. However, it's a terrible tool if you are looking for a workout plan to lose fifteen pounds. Most books that find themselves in the self-help section make promises that following their steps one through one hundred will get you exactly where you want to go. Well, I make no such promises. I know from years of reading success literature that a change in results is more about habit formation than using someone else's road map or plan.

True habit formation is learned through rigorous discipline practiced consistently over time. In contrast to rigorous discipline, every spring, thousands of golfers, myself included, head out on a journey of disappointment. We believe that after a long winter of denial, we will perform better this year than we ever have. We bought new clubs and a new putter. We bought a membership and three or four practice gadgets. We bought new tees and a wind-resistant polo shirt. We did not, however, practice at a putting facility over the winter, watch golf training videos, or hire a coach. I think at the end of this book, you will see the truth that there is only one way to improve your game, golf or otherwise, and that is by engaging in disciplined, deliberate practice.

This book explores eight thought habits and lays them out with checkpoints to help you assess where you are. Each chapter shows you where you can begin to practice the habits necessary to gain the emotional fortitude to win three battles: the battle of the head, the battle of the heart, and the battle of the hands.

Our lives are always operating in all three domains, and although we can have a life-changing insight or emotional experience or take a courageous action, none of these in isolation will bring us the result we want. We must learn to integrate the head, the heart, and the hands to achieve massive success.

Reality versus Intention

In *The Principle of the Path*, Andy Stanley lays out the truth that your direction, not your intention, determines your destination.[4] The unfortunate part about life is that many people have good intentions, but very few of the intentions reach the level of becoming actions.

The disconnect between intention and direction shows up in almost every area of life, especially when we begin making excuses for what we did or said.

Have you ever cut someone off in traffic? The natural thing to do when you realize you have cut someone off unintentionally is to, as best you can, show the person your remorse and complete penitence through apologetic hand gestures. The problem is that these gestures can easily be interpreted as hostile motions. Your intention was to drive from point A to point B uneventfully, but your action was that you accidentally cut someone off. And the fact is, no matter how repentant we may be, the person whom we've offended is carrying hostility in their heart.

Don't believe me? Think of the last time you were cut off in traffic. Do you remember the level of anger and frustration that boiled up within you? You may have wanted to bump into the other car if it didn't mean damaging your own property. There had to be some kind of way, you pondered, that you could send them the message that you were displeased.

When we see the difference between intention and action, we see that, although we judge ourselves by our intentions, we judge others almost exclusively by their actions. If you are going to break free, you have to set clear milestones and only judge your success by your achievements and not by your setting of goals.

Today versus One Day in the Future

You may be, as I used to be, approaching life and learning as if everything you learn today will have a future use or application. I thought the new ideas I learned were tools that I could put in my toolbox for one day when I was going to need them.

It took a long time for me to realize that today matters. I challenge you to choose today to learn and apply what you have learned. Below is a four-part tool I use to make my reading relevant the day I read it. This tool empowers me to put learning into practice. I expect it will do the same for you, if you use it as you read this book:

- Write your answers to all the questions at the end of the chapter.
- As a checkpoint, grade yourself and evaluate how well you feel you are currently practicing the thought habit.
- Practice the thought habit and describe your goal for it.
- Teach someone the chapter's principle within twenty-four hours of learning it.

I believe the eight thought habits in the following eight chapters will enable you to overcome personal doubts and fears to make you truly resilient!

The chapters are grouped into three sections that lay out the three battles we need to win to overcome internalized failure: the head, the heart, and the hands. Each section is an area most of my clients are battling. This book will assist you in developing your prowess in these three areas.

- The first area, the head, is the belief that we can be successful.
- The second area, the heart, is the emotional strength to move beyond feelings that have crippled us.
- The third area, the hands, is the discipline to work toward our dreams daily.

Head toward success right now by continuing to read this book.

PART I

BELIEVE THAT YOU CAN WIN

THE BATTLE OF THE HEAD

MAXIMIZING YOUR POTENTIAL

CHAPTER 3

RECOGNIZE

/ˈrekəgˌnīz/

To acknowledge the existence of[1]

Compared with what we ought to be, we are only half
awake … We are making use of only a small part of
our possible mental and physical resources.
—William James[2]

Not to give you the impression that I was a chronic dropout, but in my third and final (and successful) attempt to complete my college degree, I often played intramural football in the field across from my university. This was the place where very talented, overrated, former high school players (like me) would outshine those simply average players in order to help us cope with the truth that professional sports were not in our future.

One Saturday morning, the game was set, and we began to play all-out, no holds barred! Blood was flying, testosterone was pumping, and sweat was pouring all over the field in what could easily be described as *Gladiator* meets *Braveheart*. The sad part was that we were not playing for money, to defend our honor, or for love, family, or country. As a matter of fact, in intramural football, we didn't even get a real trophy. We simply were out there risking our bodies—and in some cases, our lives—for the sheer pleasure of saying, "We won!"

Well, all of that came crashing down for me when one of my closest friends on the team, in order to tackle someone, decided to plunge through my body in order to reach him. He hit me so hard in my thigh that I think the blood stopped flowing north to my brain. I was knocked unconscious.

When I woke up, there were a lot of concerned men around me wondering whether to call 911 and have me taken off the field by ambulance or simply drag me off the field because I was wasting precious game time. With this rude awakening, I was in a daze, unable to understand where I was or what I was doing. I felt weak and helpless, and I could not quite be sure of how quickly time was passing. I lacked the cognitive awareness to be part of an event that I should have been enjoying.

This feeling that I was not in control, that I was not fully aware of my surroundings, and that I could not define what was happening made me completely vulnerable to the suggestions of other people. People told me to take a seat, rest a bit, close my eyes, and count to ten. I followed these suggestions without much resistance, not because I wanted to, but because my weakened sense left me dependent upon the agendas of other people. What made it comical was that none of their suggestions did anything to help me.

I would like to say that this was the only time in my life when I felt such a lack of clarity, but it has not been. I've had a series of failures that has left me, at times, without the clarity and focus required to lead my own life well.

Similarly, there are millions of people who go along with the agendas of well-meaning gurus. Unfortunately, the followers have yet to become self-aware enough to take control of their own lives, and the gurus have no idea what they are talking about.

The Problems

They say, "Time flies when you are having fun." Well, time flies whether you are having fun or not! If we are not careful, very little of our lives will actually be lived. Most of us live in a haze most of the time. Have you ever been in the middle of a day and stood amazed at how quickly time has gone by? Or have you found yourself walking your daughter down the aisle only to realize you missed her childhood? What causes this lack of awareness? I see four problems that cause us to live this way. In this chapter, we'll unpack these problems and their results and then propose some solutions.

Allowing Time to Get Away from Us

As a child, I remember commenting to my uncle that sixth grade was taking forever. He responded, "The older you get, the faster time moves, especially when you have a job." Now, years later, one day seems to follow after another and another, and pretty soon, two or three days pass by without me taking note.

Andy Rooney, journalist for the television news show *60 Minutes*, quipped, "I've learned that life is like a roll of toilet paper; the closer you get to the end, the faster it goes."[3] Time is a funny thing because it is so plenteous in the mind of the youth and so valuable to those who only have a little, yet it remains the most wasted resource on the planet. We often lose time because we are not paying attention to it.

The solution to this problem is to treasure time and to pay attention to the time we have to make a difference. Time is the only thing we truly have been given. To obtain anything in our lives, we must exchange time to increase other things in our lives. We don't have money; we have time, which we exchange or leverage to earn money. We don't have loving relationships; we invest our time in people and create loving relationships. For the most part, we can have anything we want in life, but to get it, we must organize our time in the best possible way to obtain the objects of our desire.

Paying Attention to Distractions

When we are distracted, it is hard to see things clearly. When we can't see things clearly, we don't take ownership of our future. We become enslaved to our past. Countless moments are wasted thinking of things we cannot control.

Stephen Covey described this challenge by using the metaphor of two circles, one inside the other. He called the larger circle the "Circle of Concern." We see into that circle, but we cannot control all the things that happen in it. If we are consumed by concerns that we cannot influence, we lose the opportunity to take control of things we can influence.

What we can influence is what's in the smaller circle, which is called the "Circle of Influence." When we ignore things we cannot control, we decrease our frustration in the "Circle of Concern" and increase our power in our "Circle of Influence." When we do this, we can influence people and situations more effectively.[4]

Fretting and Regretting

Our culture's interest in its "Circle of Concern" is an addiction that causes stress and worry. Stress and worry immobilize us. Before we know it, months and years, holidays and seasons have flowed past us like a waterfall.

Many people spend hours reflecting on situations that neither have happened nor will happen. Or they think, "What if?" and try to change memories. The fact is, the longer we live, the more likely worry and regret will try to be our friends. However, worry and regret often drain our energy, distract us from responsibilities, and reduce our ability to change circumstances in the present time that could improve our lives now or in the future.

In particular, when we worry, our brains are trying to finish tasks. Time management expert David Allen, in *Getting Things Done*, states that open loops of unfinished tasks take a toll on our brains. Our neurocircuitry drains our attention by trying to put together unsolvable puzzles.[5]

Author David Rock, in *Your Brain at Work*, suggests that we spend 90 percent of our lives either fretting about the future or regretting the past. The challenge, he proposes, is that very little of our attention is in the present moment. Backed by neuroscientific research, he puts forward that the average person spends less than two and a half hours per day living in the present.[6]

Are you living with too many moments of worry and regret and not living in the present moment, being productive, and enjoying life? Take these two action steps to dispel the beasts of worry and regret.

Action Step 1

When you start to worry about the future, gently guide your mind into thinking about what would happen if everything turned out according to plan. Imagining a positive outcome instead of a negative one has benefits for the present and future. Watch your mood shift from anxious to excited when you imagine positive future scenarios. Imagining a positive outcome to a future event increases the likelihood that you will imagine solutions to problems you might experience along the way. Imagining a positive outcome makes it more likely that it will happen.

Action Step 2

Take your regret about a past situation and turn it into a tale of what not to do. Figure out what you need to do to not reproduce the regrettable situation in the future. Then take those ideas and create from them the steps required for success. Don't let regret overwhelm you—learn from it!

Allowing the Natural Flow of Things to Dictate Our Thoughts

Bruce Lipton cites research that paints a dismal picture. He believes that up to 90 percent of our thoughts lie below conscious awareness.[7] There is a part of the brain, referred to as the *reticular activating system*, that filters all irrelevant information out of our focus in order to conserve energy. Therefore, we find that our automatic programming drives most of our lives. If this is true, if we allow our resistance to thinking to dominate, we will be limited and never truly be in control of our lives.

The Nobel Prize–winner Albert Schweitzer was once asked, "What's wrong with people today?"

He replied, "Men simply don't think."[8]

"No brain at all, some of them [people], only grey fluff that's blown into their heads by mistake, and they don't Think," wrote A.A. Milne in *The House at Pooh Corner.*[9]

Henry Ford stated, "Thinking is the hardest work there is, which is probably the reason so few engage in it."[10]

Let's not be the topic of this disdain of the average person. Let's "wake up" and move out of the nightmare of mental inertia (to paraphrase Napoleon Hill in *Think and Grow Rich*).[11]

Wake Up

Your physical brain follows the law of entropy, which states that all things made of energy or matter degrade over time. Mental inertia will overtake our brains eventually. However, until then, let's tap into the power of our imagination, which is made from something spiritual. There is an energy within us that is more powerful than the energy of the physical, and that energy manifests as our imaginations. Humans are able to use the power of imagination to create. This spiritual power is often referred to as dreaming, but ironically, it can only happen when we are awake.

Here, I'll break up the waking or conscious dreaming into two types: *daydreaming* and *live dreaming*. Daydreaming is often reactive; it is based upon reflective thinking. It believes things happen to us and around us, but it lacks the capacity to bring forth change or adjustment.

Live dreaming is where we hold firm to the picture we're establishing—a complete image of clarity around our life vision. We're live dreaming because we're living to that vision. We're making it extremely clear and bringing it within our focus so that we have a precise understanding of what we're after. Over time, we make this vision clearer and clearer. Each step we take moves us toward it.

One of the things we're doing when we are dreaming while awake is organizing our thoughts. The organization process is most creative and fruitful if we don't restrict our thinking. In many cases, this is best accomplished when we emerge from dreaming asleep straight into a conscious dreaming state.

Many people want to wait until their thoughts are completely organized. They want to wait until they have complete clarity before they begin to move toward their dreams. The problem is that when they can't achieve total clarity, they abandon their dreams, often early on. But if we can grab hold of the vision and allow our waking hours to be consumed by moving toward that dream, then each step of moving toward that dream will bring it into clearer focus.

Are You Above or Below the Line?

In *The 15 Commitments of Conscious Leadership*, the authors talk about living above and below the line, a concept I introduced in the previous chapter.[12] They say when we're above the line, we're committed to a lifestyle in which we choose 1) not to become a victim, 2) not to allow life to just happen to us, or 3) not to be under somewhat of a trance and not recognize what's happening. So, to live above the line is to be active participants in our lives, holding our image of the future before us and moving toward it.

To live below the line is to be a victim and have a victim mindset—to be stuck in a world in which you believe you have no control over what can happen to you. People who live below the line often give up, quit, and stop expending energy. They abandon the images and the dreams they have for their future, although some will hold on to their visions as daydreams. They will not use live dreaming as a method of moving toward their dreams.

Embrace the Work of Live Dreaming

I want to reiterate something about live dreaming. Live dreaming is intentionally taking the dream that's within our hearts, within our imaginations, and creating a clear picture of it in our minds. Then we take action toward those dreams over days, weeks, months, and years.

At first, it's a lot of work to actually take an image and put it into our conscious awareness. It takes a lot of energy because the human mind only gets two and a half hours of actual thinking time a day before it needs significant rest and recovery.

Action Step

To work with this limitation, when you have a dream, think about it often at first. Spend a lot of time and mental energy creating and shaping the picture. The clearer that image becomes, the sooner you will have the power and the ability, without conscious effort, to keep it in your mind.

For example, look back at the first time you kicked a soccer ball or swung a golf club or shot a basketball. It seemed like an incredibly difficult task requiring incredibly strong motor skills. But over time, by maintaining a strong image of the result that you wanted, your body began to conform. Then your unconscious mind began to adapt and hold on to the image of what you wanted, which began to drive your behavior. This is how the dominant image ultimately drove your behavior.

Whatever image we hold, whatever dream we have, the stronger and more vibrant we make it, the more energy we put into it in the development stage, the more we will be able to sustain behavior toward it. That which took a lot of energy before becomes simple and easy over time.

The important part for us is to hold on to the image or the vision and make it so emotional and so real every day that we begin to invest our energy and actions into it naturally, without thinking.

Consider a professional golfer who can go out on the course, swing his golf club without thinking, and make a hole in one. Similarly, basketball players will often use phrases like "shooting unconsciously" or "shooting the lights out" to describe what they do on the court, meaning they're no longer in control of their shot because it's automatic. They perform this way because they have transferred the conscious process of dreaming to the subconscious or the other-than-conscious mind that follows the image, and that causes their behavior to fall in line with the image.

Part of recognizing our future is molding our image (which takes energy and thought, creativity and imagination to develop). If we emotionally buy into it and make it so powerful and so strong, it will drive our behavior. That gives us the power to overcome any obstacle or resistance.

Explore Pain and Love

Most people would live their lives half asleep. They might stay that way if it weren't for two things: pain and love. Pain causes time to slow down. If you've ever met someone who's been chronically ill, with pain coursing through their body, they'll tell you time moves extremely slowly. They are acutely aware of each moment. The second factor that can slow time down is love.

When it comes to our dreams, the pain we need to create is a dissatisfaction with the way the world is. The love we need to create is for the future—a future in which we've achieved our dreams. We have the power to take the image of the future we've created and become acutely aware of the pain that created it. At the same time, we must be deeply passionate about our vision. Those two emotions keep us awake and aware enough to move toward it.

I know a missionary serving poor people in a developing nation who often gets lost in his administrative work. The way he refreshes himself is that he often leaves his administrative duties to spend time with parents who are heartbroken because they can't feed their children or with orphans who are drinking water out of the sewer. These encounters reinvigorate the pain of why he serves the poor.

Create "Stretch" Goals

Now, for many people, when the vision is partly realized, they become comfortable and lose their passion. The way around this stagnating comfort is to create goals that stretch us. Stretch goals, benchmarks, and milestones manufacture crises. This is good in that solving those crises keeps us accelerating toward our goals.

As we challenge ourselves to be aware and recognize the world around us, we must also maintain levels of motivation and hope that keep us moving toward our goals. If we are not motivated or are unenthused by our daily work, we may be underperforming and taking longer than necessary to reach our goals.

Mihaly Csikszentmihalyi states in his book *Flow* that if we are unmotivated, if we don't have enough good stress in our lives to push us toward action, we will stay in an almost depressed state and have low performance.[13] Csikszentmihalyi shows that level as the left side or low part of a bell curve, shown in black in the figure below.

Bell Curve[14]

But, he says, if we have enough good stress, it'll push our activity up to a level of optimal performance. Csikszentmihalyi shows that level as the middle or peak of the bell curve.

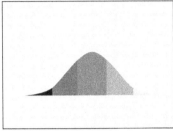

However, if we take on challenges that are hopeless or unreachable, we'll be overwhelmed, and that will push us past good stress into being overstressed. Again, we will underperform. Csikszentmihalyi shows that level as the right side or low part of a bell curve, shown in green above.

The ideal state that I want to challenge you to remain in is where you're in an optimal state of performance. You have enough stress to keep you moving toward your goals, but not so much that you are overwhelmed and stagnated.

Final Thoughts on Recognizing

Recently, I met with a friend who I had not connected with in more than fifteen years. After talking with him for about five minutes, I sensed a familiarity about his story. It turns out my long-lost friend was talking about the same dreams he had been talking about fifteen years ago. His words were still filled with enthusiasm, but he had made no progress in fulfilling his dreams. He had taken no action toward achieving them. For him, time was moving far too fast and had left him standing still.

The word *recognize* is a construction of two ideas: "re," the grammatical construct that implies a repetitive action, and "cognize," which has to do with the cognitive part of the mind, the thinking part. So, a definition for "recognize" is to raise your level of awareness of something that is already known—but possibly never acted on.

We must awaken ourselves to the fact that inaction and indecision will be cause for a less-than-satisfactory future. If we are going to achieve any degree of success in our lives, we must first become aware of the passage of time. Let me repeat: to accomplish anything significant, we must become intimately aware of the passage of time. We are unrestrained in all things except time.

Ronald Reagan declared in his first inaugural address, "We must act today in order to preserve tomorrow. And let there be no misunderstanding—we are going to begin to act, beginning today."[16] The first decision we need to make for a productive, successful future is to commit to awareness and recognize that each day is critical to our success.

There is something unique about the experience of today. The only hope we have of changing our future is changing our today.

In this chapter, we looked at the four problems that hinder self-awareness, the importance of live dreaming, the motivators of pain and love, and stretch goals.

CHAPTER 4

REFUSE

/rəˈfyo͞oz/

Show that one is not willing to do something[1]

You will become as small as your controlling
desire; as great as your dominant aspiration.
—**James Allen**[2]

The poet T. S. Eliot wrote, "Half of the harm that is done in this world is due to people who want to feel important. They don't mean to do harm … They are absorbed in the endless struggle to think well of themselves."[3] Unfortunately, these well-meaning people, often with the need to feel like experts, tend to criticize. I've experienced the negativity of these well-meaning people, in particular from a teacher in high school.

In tenth grade, I began a chemistry class in which the teacher told us students on day one that most of us would fail the class. The teacher encouraged us to drop out of his class, saying that he was paid the same no matter how many students were in his class, and if he was going to grade tests, he would prefer to only do so for a few of us. He expressed that there was a certain level of intellectual skill required for science, and he was afraid most of us didn't have it.

This was the first time I had heard a teacher say something like that out loud. However, it wasn't a surprise because the message was very familiar. By thousands of nonverbal and verbal expressions, I had heard this message loud and clear from most white teachers to students of color. I already felt I wasn't that smart due to previous academic performance, but this teacher struck a nerve. I didn't take lightly to someone challenging me. So, while many students did drop out, and the class went from thirty-three to seventeen in a matter of weeks, I stuck it out.

The first semester proved I had a lot to learn. After ending the semester with a D, I was invited to drop the course again, along with everyone who found themselves below a C. I stayed in the class. After I caught on, I found myself in a rhythm and ended the year earning an A, which the teacher was willing to replace with an Honors B so that I could enroll in Honors Physics. He was impressed with my progress. I took the Honors B and wore it like a badge of honor for refusing to believe his negativity.

Growing up, I received contradictory messages; some were encouraging and affirming, but many were negative and discouraging. Unfortunately, the negative messages have been the easiest to remember, and they powerfully changed the trajectory of my life.

The Science behind Messages

Everyone's early years are filled with messages, and at that preschool age, we process them automatically. As you may recall from chapter 1, the early phase of childhood development is known as the *delta phase* (eighteen months to five years), during which a child can absorb an unimaginable amount of information. However, when a child learns, their learning process is very different from an adult's: much of the data children take in is unfiltered.

It is during the delta phase that most of our beliefs are formed. At that age, we accept almost everything we hear without resistance because we have nothing else to compare it to. This incredible period of super-learning and downloading information is how a child in the delta phase can learn four or five languages and play three instruments without exhausting their learning. Why children don't learn more during these years has more to do with the adults in their lives being unable to keep up with them than with a limit on the children's potential.

Compare that to how an adult learns new information. When an adult learns new information, they begin by first looking for what is safe, agreeable, and familiar. Once they have categorized whether the information is to be accepted or rejected, only then will they compare the details of that information to their existing paradigms and mental models that they have developed over decades. What most people don't realize is that their mental models are almost entirely based on the messages they absorbed during their own delta childhood phase.

Around the age of five or six, alpha consciousness begins to emerge—and learning slows down considerably. If you are a parent, you will begin to hear the words "I know" from your child as he or she begins to enter the alpha phase. Those words are code for "I am an independent human who no longer needs your thoughts to make my decisions." Little do those little humans know, most of the damage of other people's negative opinions has already been done.

Early Messages Become a Frame

All of the messages we receive and accept become a frame for how we view life. We cannot underestimate the power of framing. Imagine if your plane landed in Chicago, and you were given a map of Atlantic City and a rental car with a full tank of gas and told to drive based on the map. The physical map is a frame for your journey, just as your past experiences are a frame for your life. If contradictions appeared between the map and the streets, you might not give up, but instead speed up, drive slower, or simply explain away the contradictions. You might not question whether the map is outdated or damaged.

The framing that most of us have is not an objective perspective on the world, but in many cases, it is an outdated or even damaged view of reality. The most difficult part is, if we do not challenge this outdated or damaged perspective, we become more committed to our view of being right. In many cases, we might attack and become skeptical of those who dispute our recitation of "facts," even if their views are designed to help us.

For example, I have talked to many women in physically abusive relationships. Some of them became adamant that they should stay in these relationships—even when I told them they could leave. One woman said she was willing to take a couple of punches now and then rather than be lonely. Her perspective comes from a damaged frame. She said she didn't want to be like her mother who couldn't keep a man. She couldn't see that there could be love for her that was not attached to physical violence.

You Can Reset Your Frame

The good news is, no matter what framing you begin with, you can reset it. In *First Things First*, Stephen Covey recalls a striking truth: "Between stimulus and response, there is a space. In that space is our power to choose our response."[4]

Covey suggests in *The Seven Habits of Highly Effective People* that for many people who were not raised in emotionally healthy environments that space to choose may be small, which leads to reactionary living.[5] People with small spaces don't lead their lives; their lives are controlled by the whims and ideas that emerge from others. Reactionary individuals cannot refuse the thoughts, ideas, and opinions of others concerning the choices they make.

Covey also suggests that those who grow up in healthy, supportive, and stable environments often have greater emotional resources. These privileged individuals have greater emotional awareness to consider the consequences of their actions and choose actions based on their goals. One intriguing element of Covey's work says that if we use emotional "muscles," they can become stronger. If we don't train ourselves, the emotional "muscle" will shrink.

Many people believe we stop learning at a certain age, but with all the evidence that exists concerning neural plasticity (the brain's ability to change), we know that to be false.[6] At any time, you can refuse to accept what is and begin to live a life of purpose and potential. Our mental models can be changed, poor habits can be unlearned, and our potential is only limited by our current level of awareness.

Our discipline to reframe our beliefs and attitudes relies on the practice of refusing to accept any opinion that is not in line or in harmony with the goals we have set for ourselves. I'm not saying we should immediately reject all opinions that are not in line with our goals. We need to create room for accepting other people's opinions that will improve our goals or speed up our reaching them. There should be room for discernment. When we practice the discipline of reframing our beliefs and attitude long enough, adding discernment to it becomes a skill.

Think of it like this: we are *servomechanisms*, which means that the mind directs its efforts to reach for the elements that control our focus. Our journey in life is like a heat-seeking missile aiming toward the most dominant picture we hold in our mind. This is why controlling our mental images through self-discipline is critical. We must cultivate the mental discipline of rejecting negative impressions, thus preventing negative impressions from being the guiding forces in our lives or serving as distractions from our goals.

To win against negative messaging and an outdated or damaged framework, there is a lot to consider. I'll go over five controlling forces we need to work with, work through, or work around to reframe and reach our goals.

Controlling Force 1: Negativity Bias

To compound the problem of negative messaging, we, as human beings, are disproportionately drawn to the negative things in life. When you think about it, we are sick. No matter how many good things we experience in life, the negative always stands out. I have lived in Minnesota for more than two decades, and no matter what kind of weather is outside, I hear Minnesotans complaining about it. We're attracted to the negative.

Supporting this idea is the notion of positive-negative asymmetry.[7] Think of it this way. When a child comes home and their report card has four A's and one F, where will most parents spend their time, energy, and attention? On the F. Most parents quickly glance past the four A's, the child's crowning achievement for a semester of hard work. We ignore the late nights of intense study that it must have taken our child in order to achieve the highest possible marks in four of the five classes.

The mind is set ablaze by that one mark that tells us something is wrong. We feel threatened to the core of our being that our child's future may be in jeopardy. In a split second, we become lost and uncertain—as if their failure is symbolic of a deep character flaw or a reflection of poor parenting. Were we paying attention? Did we give them too much freedom? Or is this a result of too much time in front of the television or computer screen? We lose our temper and focus it on our child. Unsure of what to say, we lash out and threaten penalties instead of celebrating the great marks while calmly asking about the one F. After all, one bad grade won't send them into a tailspin that leaves them on skid row.

Controlling Force 2: Fragile Ability to Focus

To master the art of refusing negative messages, we must understand how the mind interprets the messages it receives. The focus "muscle" is fragile and requires daily exercise. To illustrate how fragile it is, let's say I suggest to you that the tip of a fox's tail is not white. What do you see when you see the fox's tail? Most likely, you see a tail with a white tip because your thoughts and the pictures developed from those thoughts are not determined by conscious processing of logical information but by the suggested image that, although contradictory, was freely provided.

In *Your Brain at Work*, David Rock identifies the five most common elements of conscious thinking: memorizing, recalling, understanding, deciding, and inhibiting.[8] The inhibitor, which is responsible for keeping ideas out of our minds, is the weakest of the five elements. Compare the strength of the inhibitor within the human mind. It's the brakes of a ten-speed bike put on an eighteen-wheeler semi-truck. Metaphorically speaking, we need to turn those bike brakes into powerful semi-truck air brakes. We must develop the inhibitor "muscle" needed to reject the ideas that create negative images that stop us from reaching our goals.

Action Step

Think of a time in your life when you've experienced the following negative messages. Then take some time to refute the negative messages with positive ones.

- A hateful word, which can inflict self-hatred.
- An inappropriate touch, which can diminish value and self-respect.
- Constant verbal reprimands, which can lead to low self-image.
- A disparaging remark, which can lead to long-term resentment.

- Exposure to violence firsthand or secondhand, which leads to anger and guilt.

Controlling Force 3: Competing Values

Most people are quick to compromise their dreams because there is very little about their future they are actually committed to. Deep within your heart, there must be a resounding yes that drowns out all things that would pose a threat to your ultimate goal. This resolve is not generated overnight; it is developed as you tap into the depths of your true values.

We have inconsistent values because life is not a fight between good and bad values. Instead, it is an endless series of decisions about an endless hierarchy of conflicting values. It is only when we are internally conflicted that we begin to see in what order these values fall. All too often, human nature guides us to avoid conflict—so we live a life unable to establish a strong enough yes. While we should refuse to accept anything less than our vision, we crumble and settle for average. One of the most fundamental reasons people don't use the power of refusal to hone their life's purpose and direction is because they are resistant to going through the painstaking process of determining what is truly essential.

Humans are needy creatures. Acknowledging this is the first step in coming to grips and moving past this reality. It is a difficult feat to wrestle through insecurities we developed as children. To strive toward success, it is difficult to extract ourselves from negative relationships, especially when they are also our closest relationships. As mentioned before, rejection is such a powerful blow to the ego that many people cannot face it. Many people spend their lives trying to avoid the penalty of rejection they experienced in grade school, middle school, or high school. They are busy trying not to disappoint or offend people who are no longer looking.

We must refuse to be directed by others. Deep within our hearts, we must develop a deep commitment to purpose and refuse to accept failure as an option. This choice to know our purpose, grow to our potential, and sow seeds that benefit others must be so resolute that it gives us the emotional fortitude to embrace the consequences of saying no to things that get in the way. This strength does not come all at once; it is developed over time.

If you allow life to shape you, it will lead you to the path of least resistance. This path will put you at the bottom of the ocean. It will make you into the softest substance, mold you into the most convenient shape, and melt you into the most pliable material. What you've become—clay—has little value.

In contrast, diamonds are extremely valuable. To become a diamond, you must force yourself to harden when others try to melt you, resist when others try to shape you, and fight when others try to mislabel you, even if such actions cause you to be separated from your family and friends.

In *The Dream Giver*, Bruce Wilkinson suggests that everyone has a dream, and at some point, we must leave the town of the familiar in the land of the ordinary to face dream killers (border bullies) who are often those closest to us.[9] Whether we are children or full-grown adults, the greatest enemies our dreams face are often close family members and friends. The truth is, we must reframe and refuse to allow them to hold us back.

Controlling Force 4: Conflicting Commitments

Motivational speaker Brian Tracy asserts, "You can make excuses or you can make progress. You choose."[10] It is incredibly important as we talk about the power of refusal to address our competing commitments. As a leadership coach, I have heard so many "good excuses" from well-meaning executive clients. In twenty years of consulting, I've seen firsthand that leaders who don't make excuses are the ones who find a way to their goals.

I realize that what I am about to say is controversial, but as Proverbs 27:6 says, "Faithful are the wounds of a friend."[11] We must have authentic relationships with others and ourselves that require us to be honest about who we are and what is required of us as we seek to fulfill our purpose.

Many people find, when reviewing how they spend their time that they have been lying to themselves about what they want. They find they have been spending a lot of time on activities that are unrelated to their goals. They find that once they align their activities with their goals, they are calmer and progress toward their goals faster. As John Maxwell says, "The secret of your success is determined by your daily agenda."[12]

Another hard truth about commitments is that they take significant energy. As Andy Stanley puts it, "Devoting a little of yourself to everything means committing a great deal of yourself to nothing."[13] In other words, to reach your goals, you must focus your mind and energy.

Constant activity has the deceptive nature of making us feel as if we are accomplishing something. Activity itself is not progress. If the actions you are taking are not intentionally leading you to something meaningful, then you may just be spinning your wheels. It's like the old joke where the airplane pilot announces that he has good news and bad news. The good news is they are making great time; the bad news is they have no idea where they are.

Controlling Force 5: Refusing a Permission-Based Life

My closest and most enduring friendship is with a man by the name of Clifton Ross, and he is stupid. Now, when I told him that I was putting this sentence in this book, he told me that it may cost me our friendship. However, when I explained what I meant by stupid, he actually agreed with me. When I say stupid, I am referring to the dictionary definition, which is "the lack of *ordinary* quickness and keenness of mind."

Now, Clifton is extremely sharp, incredibly talented, and charismatic, but he suffers—and I dare say he suffers intentionally—in his unwillingness to engage with people's micro aggressions. He does not relinquish his volition to others, even when they attempt to deny him permission to move forward toward his goals.

I remember his years building a successful Amway business. He was committed to approaching five people a day to join his team—in spite of people's clear indications at first that they didn't want him anywhere near them. His opening line was this: "Are you excited by what you do—or are you keeping your options open?" During his sales pitch, some people would forcefully reject him.

When we extrapolate what's really happening, it's actually that the person doesn't trust themself not to buy more than they have in their budget, and so their aggression is to reject or fend off anybody who will try to seduce them or manipulate them or take advantage of them. So, at the heart of people's resistance is a sense of insecurity and fear of being taken advantage of. As consumers, we consistently demonstrate this method of protecting ourselves by rejecting the salesperson. This goes back to the beginning of the chapter and what T. S. Eliot said about half the harm being done in this world being done not because people want to do harm but because they simply are in an endless struggle to feel good about themselves.

For these two reasons alone, we have to be careful about how we view rejection. If we accept people's rejection, and it causes us to reshape our behaviors, we will find ourselves conforming to a permission-based life.

Clifton refuses to live a permission-based life. He refuses to wait for other people's permission in order to move forward. Let's see how this helped him reach his goal of business success.

Ever since we were in high school, Clifton has had a strong drive for success. He initially went to college after high school, but during his first year, he looked around at his network of people with all their bachelor's, master's, and doctoral degrees and could not find one person leading a successful business, so he quit college.

At nineteen years old, Clifton went into a Hilton Hotel, intending to apply for an entry-level job. He noticed that there was a supervisor position open three levels higher, so he applied for that instead. He was hired within a week.

Several months later, the hiring manager found out Clifton's age and asked, "What gave you the courage to apply for that position?"

He said, "Because it was available."

Most people wouldn't have dared to take those steps. They would have applied for the entry-level position and waited for permission from management to move up to supervisor.

But, you see, Clifton was too stupid (refused) to accept a socially expected entry-level position when a higher position was available, so he applied for the supervisor position. And he carried with him a confident demeanor that landed him his first three jobs that "required" a degree he didn't have.

You see, at a young age, Clifton worked in a multilevel marketing business that suggested that if the people who are successful in the field you want to enter have degrees, you should follow in their footsteps. Clifton wanted to be successful in business, and he quickly learned that most people who were leading the charge in business had barely graduated from college, had no college degree, or didn't even have a high school diploma. So, he stopped going to college and surrounded himself with mentors who essentially taught him what they knew—not to be put off by people's natural sense of resistance—and he became successful in business.

Dallas Willard says that rejection is the strongest human impulse, and the thousands of micro aggressions we experience every day tell us to conform to mediocrity.[14] If we conform, we're protecting and shielding ourselves from people's rejection, but we're denying ourselves the success that we ultimately could have.

We have to learn to catch a case of stupid, which means to numb our senses to the opinions of others and move forward toward the goals we set for ourselves. That's what Clifton did, but if you ask him, he'll say he just got lucky.

Simple logic would have told him to stick with the hotel supervisor job he was "lucky" to have, but he couldn't believe that working for someone else would allow him to achieve the results he was seeking. So, he quit and began working for a mortgage company. In two years, he made almost half a million dollars, and then he bought out the company.

He made quite a bit of money in his newfound leadership role, but that all came crashing down when the housing market bottomed out in 2008. At that point, it would have been easy to give up and settle for a job offered by a headhunter: a job that would have taken care of his family. Again, he was too stupid (refused). He decided he would rather go broke than work for someone else.

He began another business with four partners. This business has revolutionized estate planning in Minnesota. His success is due to the fact that he was too stupid (refused) to listen and respond to other people's opinions. Clifton is more than my stupid best friend; he is an example to me and many other leaders he has mentored over the years.

Another one of my heroes and mentors, John Maxwell, says the secret to his success is high energy and low IQ. He claims that if he were smarter, he would never have been able to succeed because he would have talked himself out of doing the right things for success.[15]

Are you too smart for your own good? Do you talk yourself out of doing the right things for success? You are in luck. Here are five things you can do to be less smart—in other words, to be stupid and reap the benefits of it:

Things for You to Refuse in Order to Succeed

1. Refuse Urgency

Western business culture facilitates people fulfilling urges. For example, scrolling on the phone, answering emails, and attending meetings cater to a desire for easy, convenient work.

However, true productivity requires us to resist urges and instead focus on completing tasks that will prevent crises. Responding to urgency provides us with a sense of achievement, but it reduces our focus on our goals. We must embrace the anthem that activity is not equal to progress. The danger of responding to urgent activity is that it provides many people with a sense of purpose without actually doing anything that moves them toward their goals.

Henry David Thoreau wrote:

> If one advances confidently in the direction of his dreams, and endeavors to live the life which he has imagined, he will meet with a success unexpected in common hours. He will put some things behind, will pass an invisible boundary; new, universal, and more liberal laws will begin to establish themselves around and within him; or the old laws be expanded, and interpreted in his favor in a more liberal sense, and he will live with the license of a higher order of beings.[16]

This ability to meet with "success, unexpected in common hours," suggests that our intentional, purposeful, and visionary movements will help us hurdle our invisible barriers to achieve what we previously thought impossible.

2. Refuse Negative Attitudes

Your attitude is the way in which you meet and greet the world. Attitudes are correlated with perspective. Some people greet the world with passion, optimistic expectation, and positive ideas, and this energizes their drive. Others enter their day with fear, anxiety, and skepticism, which hastens their defeat. Both of these types of people are controlled by their attitudes.

Watching movies is something I do for recreation. Growing up, I used to go to movies all by myself just to stay current. Over the years, very few movies have drawn my tears, but I must admit that one movie on my sob list is *Forrest Gump*. People love this movie because Forrest was the luckiest man that ever lived except when it came to love.[17]

For anyone who hasn't seen the movie, Forrest was a little slower than most children, but his mother instilled within him a naiveté that allowed him to accept his situation. Forrest kept a positive attitude and thought the best of people. He gave them the benefit of the doubt—even and especially when they couldn't see the good in themselves.

Forrest oversimplified and solved problems that common sense would have told him to stay away from. For example, as a child, he walked in leg braces, and people often asked him what was wrong with his feet. His response was simple, soft-spoken, and charming: "Nothing, doctor says my legs are strong as an ox, but my back is as crooked as an arrow."[18] Therefore, since his legs were fine, for him that solved the problem.

Sometimes it's not our situation that hinders us, but our negative attitudes about our situations. But take heart—like Forrest Gump, you really do have a choice about your attitude. People may control your situation, but no one but you is responsible for how you perceive it.

Practical Tip

You may not meet all the qualifications in a job posting, but don't let that stop you from applying for a position you want. Be like my friend Clifton—and don't assume you are underqualified. Qualifications on a job posting are usually cut and pasted from a template. Most organizations want to see results over platitudes on a resume, but few organizations have done the deep work to determine a good fit beyond a simple job description. Know your strengths and how they apply to the job. Present your strengths and see what happens!

3. Refuse Negative People

Have you ever met someone who tends to find the dark clouds but not the silver linings, always sees the glass as half empty, and—despite having no expertise of their own—sounds like a professional critic when it comes to every aspect of life? You probably have. But have you ever stopped to think how miserable a life like that is—to ensure that everyone else sees the worst in life?

What I am about to say may sound terrible, but it is absolutely critical to successful living: You have to "put them out!" A story in the Bible illustrates this principle. In Luke 8, there is a wonderful story about Jesus bringing a little girl back from death. When Jesus arrives at the child's house, he says that the girl is not dead but only asleep. After hearing the derision of his statement from the people in the house, Jesus puts them all out and brings the girl back to life.[19]

Are people belittling your dreams? At some point, as a dreamer, you will come to a time when you will need people of faith around you, as Jesus needed his disciples. Then you will have the strength to deal with those who are belittling your dreams. Your response should be as firm as Jesus's was with the doubters in the girl's house: He kicked them out. Likewise, you have to kick out naysayers and disgruntled associates from your inner circle because they will kill your momentum and positive energy.

4. Refuse Negative Outcomes

You will be challenged, and you will fail! Those are natural parts of life. As mentioned earlier, there are three things that shape each of our lives: being accepted, being rejected, and our response. You must develop the ability to refuse to be stopped by that which challenges you.

You must take on the attitude of one who refuses to lose. You need a gut check that makes you hard as nails. You must become the type of person who knows what they want. You must dodge whatever traps are out there.

In the words of Benjamin Disraeli, "Nothing can resist the human will that will stake even its existence on its stated purpose."

5. Refuse Negative Decisions

As I mentioned in chapter 2, the first time I interviewed for the top leadership position in an organization, I was declined. I had been the number two guy for years, and I was serving as interim president: giving vision, leadership, and direction while waiting on the board of directors to hire the next leader. As I mentioned earlier, from my point of view, I was the clear favorite for the position.

I had been with the organization for more than seven years and had the full support of the staff. Due to my longevity with the organization, I knew the history and the people we were serving. I was truly the only one who could lead the organization immediately without onboarding or training.

But the board of directors rejected me for the position—not once but twice. I refused to give in to their limited understanding of what the organization needed. I gave even more of myself under the new leadership in order to make sure that the organization would be perfectly ready for me when I assumed the leadership role.

I ultimately was appointed leader of the organization because I refused to accept no for an answer. I had to work in a lower capacity for a time, but the closed door to the position of president eventually became a bridge to me officially leading the organization.

Final Thoughts on Refusing

You must accept the fact that you have more control over your future than any circumstance you face. Like a powerful river, you can be redirected, but you cannot be stopped. Grab onto the confidence that arises within you. Accept the power of who you can be versus how you have been viewed in the past, perhaps even by yourself.

If you want to be successful, you have to learn to block out every-thing that leads you to believe you can't. The alternative to moving forward is a slow but certain death. People who live without a pas-sionate pursuit of their dreams are already dead and just awaiting a funeral to make it official.

As we grow up, our parents, teachers, peers, coaches, and even enemies give us messages about who we are and how much we can accomplish. These messages are both positive and negative and come in various forms. They shape the way we view ourselves.

For example, my African American friend Karen received many negative messages growing up in the inner city. A store owner told her that she couldn't buy from his store because they didn't sell to "little nigger girls." From him, she learned that she was the wrong color. Her schoolmates harped on her looks. From them, she learned she was ugly. Fellow students didn't want to spend time with a book-worm. From them, she learned that her friendship was not valued. A teacher refused to let her enroll in woodshop. From him, she learned that she was the wrong gender.

After all was said and done, if Karen had listened to all those messages from her childhood and adolescence, she would not be Reverend Dr. Karen McKinney today. She has been all over the world, including Palestine, to attempt to negotiate peace between the Jews and the Palestinians. Reverend Dr. McKinney is one of the most revered teachers on experiential learning in the world today and currently serves the governor of Minnesota as the diversity di-rector of the Department of Human Services.

Like Karen, you must develop a rejection button for negative press. You cannot allow your mind to be contaminated with the lies of other people's negative opinions about you.

However, most of us have trouble rejecting negative messaging because the messages are often so subtle that we experience the rejec-tion before we can react to what is being communicated. Sometimes it's as subtle as someone chuckling when you ask to participate in a competition that they feel you are unqualified for. Or you might internalize the rejection you hear in the disdainful voice of someone you respect. Even the quick dismissal of your request for a promotion can be a rejection. All these factors can send messages to the psyche and cripple your ability to grow and produce on a higher level.

I hope this chapter has taught you that, with mental practice, you can overcome negative messages and a negative framework. The benefit is personal growth, which leads to greater happiness and success.

CHAPTER 5

RESOLVE

/rəˈzälv/

Firm determination to do something[1]

Determination gives you the resolve to keep going
in spite of the roadblocks that lay before you.
—Denis Waitley[2]

I have only been skiing once in my life. I was thirteen years old, and my church youth group leaders decided to take our youth group from the inner city of Chicago out to try skiing for the first time. It was really a lesson in how to die in snow.

There is no way I can do this, I thought when we arrived at the ski hill. I felt small when I looked up at the huge hill from the bottom. The group leaders had brought us out there with no instruction on this dangerous sport. The windy night was no help; it provided subzero weather.

Nevertheless, I ventured out as I always did in order to prove my newfound independence as a teenager. I ran into a member of my youth group who was known as "the girl with the boy name" (Jeffery). Because she was nineteen—what I thought was a mature age—I felt I needed to act mature to impress her. I asked, "Do you want to join me on the ski lift?" To my pleasure, she agreed.

Now there were two of us going up the ski lift, excited to try out skiing for the first time. After about five minutes, we became mildly nervous because there was no sign of the end of the ride. The full ride to the top was thirty minutes. At the top, we were nervous wrecks because we didn't know how we were going to get down the hill. We tried what we went there for. We skied down the first three slopes, but we kept falling on our butts.

After that, I decided it would be safer if I stayed closer to the ground in order to reduce the distance of the fall. I soon discovered that the lower I was to the ground, the faster I went down the hill—and the faster I went down the hill, the more painfully the air ripped at my face. After a dozen more falls, we gave up. We were scared because we had no idea how long it would take us to walk down the hill in the freezing weather.

My desires to hide my fear and still be a gentleman manifested when I offered to carry Jeffery's skis down the hill along with my own. I didn't care that I looked ridiculous carrying four skis twice as long as my body, but I was walking slowly. After we walked down one slope, Jeffery grabbed her skis and took off without me. About fifteen minutes later, I saw her skis sticking out of the snow with no Jeffery in sight. I walked for another twenty minutes before abandoning my skis as well.

That was the first time in my life I had no idea where I was or how long it would take me to get back to safety. I began to think that I wouldn't make it, that everyone would tell the story of the kid who got on the ski lift (even though he couldn't ski) and froze to death.

There are life-changing moments in a person's life, and this was one of them for me. I decided that no matter what, I would not be found dead on the side of a mountain. I didn't know what to do, and there was no one I could call for help, but I could put one foot in front of the other until I arrived at the chalet. I was determined to live. Three hours after getting on that ski lift, I made it back. Upon my return, one of the chaperones asked, "How was the bunny hill?" I must have looked like death because he quickly added, "Never mind."

How Strong Is Your Desire?

Events often mark important milestones in our lives. Each of these markers provides an opportunity to renew our resolve. Events such as birthdays, anniversaries, and New Year's Eve give us the chance to proclaim declarations, make commitments, and attempt to shift direction. We hope through these new commitments to establish better outcomes for our lives.

New Year's resolutions help establish a turning point from which we can change our behavior. We believe that a behavior change will deliver to us a specific result, but we often have not clearly established the specific outcome we want. Instead, we are mostly focused on a behavior we want to eliminate. This shift is often driven by a hope, a wish, or a want, and not a true desire.

Napoleon Hill states in *Think and Grow Rich*:

> There is a difference between *wishing* for a thing and being *ready* to receive it. No one is ready for a thing until he believes he can acquire it. The state of mind must be *belief*, not mere hope or wish. Open-mindedness is essential for belief.[3]

When we want something but lack the emotional commitment or resolve to actually follow through to the end, we break faith with our wish. That failure makes it less likely we'll fully commit to achieving it the next time.

Similarly, when we position ourselves to achieve a goal, we cannot enter from a place of lack or want. When the goals we set are from a place of struggle, we experience negative imagery in our minds and negative emotions in our hearts. This imagery shrouds the positive imagery and emotions we need to radiate the energy required to maintain a level of resolve to achieve success.

By operating from a place of want and lack, we assume there is not enough of something in the world. Either there is not enough of the things we desire—or we don't have enough skill and ability to achieve it. Maybe there's not enough support or not enough resources to maintain a high level of commitment. For those difficult times, consider the words of Ambrose Bierce, nineteenth-century American journalist: "Who never doubted, only half believed. Where doubt is, there truth is—it is her shadow."[4]

For many people, when they recognize they want something, they assume wanting it is enough. They may evaluate all the external factors that have inhibited their previous success because they believe the challenges are only external. For example, on January 1, they get a new planner, purchase a gym membership, choose a new diet program, buy a personal development program, or choose a new book from Oprah's list. On average, twenty-seven days later, they don't even remember the goals they committed to. They abandon their plan primarily because it wasn't based on a "burning desire"[5] but on a lightly held want.

When we pursue lightly held wants, we often have an on-again, off-again mentality. We go in spurts because our commitment to our dreams is not strong enough to provide the stamina for continued pursuit.

> A goal casually set and lightly taken is freely
> abandoned at the first obstacle.
> **—Zig Ziglar**[6]

In *Think and Grow Rich*, Napoleon Hill reinforced the necessity of having a burning desire or an all-consuming obsession to reach success.[7] This means becoming resolute and committing to a solution that is not based in want and wish but in true desire. There's a difference between wanting something and having a specific purpose with a definite plan.

When you're working on your plan, and your work, your effort, your focus, and your purpose become a dominating obsession, you'll feel the difference. It's different than saying, "I really want it." You'll say instead, "I really need it. I'm determined. Nobody wants it more than me." If you are going to break through, your goal must become an obsession.

Go High to Jump

When a skydiver commits to jumping out of a plane, the worst mistake he or she can make is not flying high enough. The most dangerous thing is to jump from too low a height. Jumping from a lower height may appear safer because they don't have so far to go, right? But you want to be way up high when you pull that chute because you want the time to prepare for a safe landing. Similarly, one of my mentors shared with me that only by dreaming big and playing all-out can you be sure of maintaining that burning desire that is so essential to success.

I'm willing to bet that the reason most people fail is because they play it safe. They don't have a big enough dream that requires them to get to a high level of intensity. Their dream doesn't require that they risk anything, that they burn their bridges, or that they go from wanting to all-consuming, burning obsession. They never risk it all by betting on themselves. They cheat themselves out of the growth that comes from putting themselves in a position that forces them to give their best efforts toward a goal. Personal growth brings success, and success brings more personal growth. Most people overestimate the risk and underestimate their potential.

Most people fail in life not because they aim too high
and miss, but because they aim too low and hit.
—Les Brown[8]

Your Context Matters

Dr. Paul R. Scheele is a world-renowned thought leader from whom I have had the privilege of receiving mentorship for the past several years. He created a Natural Brilliance Model based on four quadrants: *present positive, present negative, future negative,* and *future positive.*[9] I believe this model perfectly describes the process of breaking through struggle.

The Four Quadrants of the Natural Brilliance Model

Quadrant 1: Present Positive

This quadrant represents the comfort zone: the place many struggling people are trying to get to. Many people are suffering from discontent because they are playing the lottery of life, hoping that something happens that will make things just a little bit better. In this quadrant, people try to get the most out of today rather than counting the cost and paying the price for tomorrow. Their focus is on doing whatever it takes to ensure they remain comfortable. In this quadrant, people strive to eliminate risk, resistance, and discomfort.

Most thought leaders, like Napoleon Hill, advise the opposite:

> Every person who wins in any undertaking must be willing to burn his ships and cut all sources of retreat. Only by so doing can one be sure of maintaining that state of mind known as a burning desire to win, essential to success.[10]

Quadrant 2: Present Negative

This quadrant is a place that we all must be careful not to get caught in. When we get comfortable, many of us start feeling entitled. When we feel entitled, we start to complain.

Call it Minnesota, but I have heard more people complain about the weather than anything else in the decades that I have lived in this state. We have strange weather patterns, without a doubt, but there is nothing more futile than complaining about what you cannot change. Yet for some reason, this futility gives people solace.

Complaining is the language of defeat; it is an acknowledgement of powerlessness and victimhood. The sad thing is that billions of people don't have consistent nutrition or predictable meals, and yet millions of Americans, rather than being grateful for what they have, complain about the taste and texture of their food. We complain because we feel victimized when we get less than we feel entitled to receive. We must break out of quadrant 2 and the custom of complaining—and engage instead in the power of gratitude. We'll cover the true power of gratitude in our next chapter.

Quadrant 3: Future Negative

If there is one thing that keeps us running away from the dreams in our hearts, it is the fear in our heads. There is no doubt a risk in pursuing your dream, but the risk of standing still is even greater. The doubts and concerns of failure, rejection, and loss can dominate our thoughts while creating images of shame and embarrassment.

This quadrant tends to be full of people who have achieved a modicum of success. This is because once people experience a win, many of them stop improving, stop taking risks, and attempt to live in the glory of previous success.

William Pollard wrote, "The arrogance of success is to think that what you did yesterday will be sufficient for tomorrow."[11] We can't afford to bask in the glow of yesterday's victories. This doesn't mean we don't celebrate a win. We do celebrate, but then we move on to new goals.

I coach entrepreneurs. An entrepreneur is someone who, by definition, has to take risks and bet on themself to start their business.

They often sacrifice meals, sleep, big purchases, and retirement accounts for the purpose of fulfilling their dreams of leading their own companies. One of the biggest downfalls I've seen is when they want to graduate from the role of entrepreneur and simply move to the role of business owner. I challenge this thinking because there is no nirvana called "Business Owner Land."

When business owners stop risking, growing, and challenging themselves, their businesses begin to suffer. This suffering often causes the entrepreneur to retreat from professional growth because they are afraid of failing and starting over. They call it "being smart." Unfortunately, the greatest threat to tomorrow's success is yesterday's success. We need to abandon quadrant 3, stop thinking about what might go wrong, and learn to live in the fourth and final quadrant.

Quadrant 4: Future Positive

As you can imagine, the other three quadrants dominate the thinking of most people. This last quadrant requires a lot of mental focus to live in. We must commit a great amount of mental toughness to build the internal strength and emotional fortitude to stay dedicated to our dreams. The future positive is the vision that we must write down and make plain so that when others see it, they can understand it and join us.

In *Visioneering*, Andy Stanley gives my favorite definition of vision: "Vision is a clear mental picture of what could be, fueled by the conviction that it should be."[12] If the picture is going to be clear, we have to put in the work to make it so.

I believe that we all have been endowed with purpose, passion, and a vision that can make the world a better place to live. It's been said that the problems that frustrate you the most are the ones you were meant to solve. This means that paying attention to the things that bother you, excite you, and awaken your passion may be the path to discovering your purpose.

A Clear and Definite Goal

While *character* is the substance of who we are underneath, our thought habits are the results of our character. Thought habits turn into decisions, which turn into actions toward or away from our goals.

Every client I have ever worked with at some level had a dream, a desire, a clear goal, or a preferred future. When we begin our coaching relationship, we first try to develop clarity surrounding what they are trying to achieve. Upon closer inspection, we discover the struggle is rarely about being uncertain about what they want. Instead, I find that my clients are constantly wrestling with competing commitments that distract and divert them from what they desire.

This internal wrestling creates internal conflicts that produce uncertainty, and this uncertainty causes my clients to revisit problems that were already solved. Coping with competing commitments is a difficult task to take on alone. This is where coaching becomes invaluable for my clients. I tell them, "Once you solve something, it is incredibly important that you develop the resolve to stick with that solution." When something is solved, you don't go and try to renegotiate with it.

We're Drowning in Knowledge

Wouldn't it be great if human behavior was primarily based on knowledge? As we learn better, we would do better. John Maxwell says, "The greatest gap in the world is the gap between knowing and doing."[13]

There's a lot of knowledge in the world. President Bill Clinton said in his 1998 State of the Union address that the storehouse of knowledge doubles every five years.[14] Now, it is estimated that what we know is doubling every twelve hours.[15] So, when it comes to what is needed to drive change, I hope it is clear that the amount of knowledge is not the problem.

For example, I know how to lose weight, I know how to make more money, and I know how to set goals—but that's not enough. The problem is not setting goals; it is developing skills in goal achievement. It is not difficult to dream; the challenge comes in living out that dream. When we consider the amount of money spent on education, there is no doubt all the problems of the world would be solved if knowledge were the solution.

> I fear not the man who has practiced ten
> thousand kicks once, but I fear the man who has
> practiced one kick ten thousand times.
> **—Bruce Lee**[16]

The commitment, the mental resolve to focus on a specific task, is the key to moving ourselves out of average and into action. It bears repeating: our lives are a result of our actions, our actions a result of our decisions, our decisions a result of our thought habits, and our thought habits a result of our character, which directs and determines our lives. If we don't understand this series of connections, we find ourselves using much of our energy to complete an endless bid to improve our performance rather than engaging in a process of becoming a better overall performer.

Nathan Nolan, in his short story "Memento Mori," gives us insight into the human psyche, which shows that humans lie victim to their current state of mind. The passage gives me hope that we can do better when we follow a plan to reach a goal:

> We're all at the mercy of the limbic system, clouds
> of electricity drifting through the brain. Every man
> is broken up into twenty-four-hour fractions, and
> then again within those twenty-four hours. It's a
> daily pantomime, one man yielding control to the

next: a backstage crowd with old hacks clamoring for their turn in the spotlight. Every week, every day. The angry man hands the baton over to the sulking man, and in turn to the sex addict, the introvert, the conversationalist. Every man is a mob, a chain gang of idiots.

This is the tragedy of life. Because for a few minutes of every day, every man becomes a genius. Moments of clarity, insight, whatever you want to call them. The clouds part, the planets get in a neat little line, and everything becomes obvious. I should quit smoking, maybe, or here's how I can make a fast million, or such and such is the key to eternal happiness. That's the miserable truth. For a few moments, the secrets of the universe are opened to us ...

But the genius, the savant, has to hand over the controls to the next guy down the pike, most likely the guy who just wants to eat potato chips, and insight and brilliance and salvation are all entrusted to a moron or a hedonist or a narcoleptic. The only way out of this mess, of course, is to take steps to ensure that you control the idiots that you become. To take your chain gang, hand in hand, and lead them. It's like a letter you write to yourself. A master plan, drafted by the guy who can see the light, made with steps simple enough for the rest of the idiots to understand. Follow steps one through one hundred. Repeat as necessary.[17]

It's not enough to take action toward our goals. We need character, a change in thought habits, decisions that support our goals, a well-thought-out plan, and resolve to push change into being.

Mining Resolve

Crunch time. Moment of truth. High noon. Do you know if you have enough resolve to push through your next pivotal point? James Allen shows you how to find out:

> Only by much searching and mining are gold and diamonds obtained, and man can find every truth connected with his being if he will dig deep into the mine of his soul; and that he is the maker of his character, the molder of his life, and the builder of his destiny, he may unerringly prove, if he will watch, control, and alter his thoughts, tracing their effects upon himself, upon others, and upon his life and circumstances, linking cause and effect by patient practice and investigation, and utilizing his every experience, even to the most trivial, everyday occurrence, as a means of obtaining that knowledge of himself which is Understanding, Wisdom, Power.[18]

Changing our results starts with knowing our character.

The Erosion of Resolve

Psychologist Jonathan Haidt describes a popular psychological concept known as "the divided self" in *The Happiness Hypothesis*.[19] We, as humans, are not simply a monolith of desires, choices, and character. We have desires that often conflict and compete with one another. One side of our personality may have incredible resolve in certain situations while the other, depending on the situation, may overpower it.

The belief that willpower alone can change results is an unfortunate myth that leaves most people ill-equipped to provide defense from decisions that lead down destructive paths. The most important part of understanding the divided self, the conflicted self, the distracted self is understanding what happens when we give up control and weaken our resolve.

The Rider and the Elephant

The human mind is often described as being two very powerful but distinct operating systems: the *cognitive mind* and the *emotional mind*. Ages ago, Buddha taught about this distinction of the two minds by giving us the analogy of the rider and the elephant.

The Rider

The rider represents our cognitive mind, the part of us that dictates our will, makes our decisions, and filters the important out of the mundane. The cognitive mind or conscious mind has the power to think about thinking (metacognition.) This part of the mind also gives us the power to reflect, plan, create, adjust, set goals, and even restrain our impulses when evaluating their consequences. The rider's unique ability to inhibit, recall, memorize, decide, and understand is what makes us uniquely human. David Rock says, "The rider empowers us to advance the cause of our life or evolve the social condition of a generation."[20]

The rider part of the brain does not come without its challenges. Its strength is its unique ability to lead and direct the human experience, but its weaknesses are its small size, limited strength, and lack of ability to stay engaged. Although the rider is extremely powerful, it has less sustained energy than that of a lion, which is said to sleep for twenty hours a day. The rider can only do so many things at full strength, and moving in more than one direction at the same time is not possible. Rock said, "The mind of a Harvard graduate can be turned into that of an eight-year-old if asked to do two things at once."[21]

The rider is also very fragile and self-conscious. They can be derailed by fear, insults, stress, or anything that suggests that any part of the ego is in danger (whether the threat is perceived or real). The slightest threat causes the rider to turn over the controls to the elephant, which is known as our default nature. If we are to succeed in overpowering our default nature, we have to build a structure that helps us direct our elephant and remain in control.

The Elephant

Our emotional mind can be a great asset or a ticking time bomb, depending on the task we are asking it to complete. The elephant represents our emotional self, and like any elephant, it never forgets, and it is easy to excite and difficult to control when excited. Although we may struggle with recalling knowledge on a dime, emotional memory is a permanent fixture in our minds. The emotional mind records every memory and responds with an exactness of impulse based on its programming.

When I was in college, I worked in retail, and I wondered why, after Thanksgiving, the owner wanted us to put pine and peppermint air freshener plug-ins in the store. Amazingly enough, people began to smile and purchase more. I realized the smells of pine and peppermint remind people of the Christmas season, which for their emotional recall center, is positive. As it is forecast in the song, "It's the most wonderful time of the year."

It's not just Christmas that brings strong feelings. For many people, anniversaries of personal traumas and tragedies mark seasons and times of the year that can plunge us into a deeply emotional state. An anniversary of the loss of a child can cause profound grief for parents, sometimes so profound that the parents cannot bear to see each other and end their marriage. The elephant is directing their lives.

Events can cause feelings to manifest in the body: "Given how closely the gut and brain interact, it becomes easier to understand why you might feel nauseated before giving a presentation or feel intestinal pain during times of stress."[22] The elephant has taken over.

Direct the Rider, Motivate the Elephant, and Shape the Path

So, how does knowing about the rider and elephant enable us to strengthen our resolve? I'd like to introduce you to the framework of two of my favorite writers, Dan and Chip Heath. These authors have helped me and many of my clients understand how to create a vision that is "sticky." A "sticky" vision leads to a sustainable increase in resolve. In their book *Switch*, they lay out a framework that has been so helpful to me, I want to present it for you here.[23]

Direct the Rider

Do the work, take control of the narrative in your head, and lay out a clear plan with a clear destination. Our ability to sustain a clear picture and direction for our cognitive mind often boils down to the intentional direction we claim over our narrative circuitry.

Most people, when having a debate, find that their points of contention have less to do with the facts and more to do with the story they tell themselves about the facts. No two narratives are identical, although close relationships can transmit empathy. Each person carries a story, and their version of the facts informs their behavior.

Most people have more than one competing voice in their heads. If a person has been abused in a work relationship and still must interact with people daily at work, they might have to contend with a voice in their head that says, "I deserve to be abused." Another voice might say, "People will like me for who I am and treat me with respect." Neither voice is objective; it bases its version of the conversation on relevant needs, desires, and life experiences.

The way we change the result of being the target of an abusive person is to look at what in our character attracts the abuser. Do we spend time in lonely places? Are we meek until we can't take any more verbal abuse, and then we lash out verbally? If we change our character, the result is that only one picture in our head remains: that we don't deserve the abuse. We may even change our thoughts so far as to believe we deserve to be around people who love and respect us. The mental clutter resulting from abuse disappears because our thought patterns have changed.

Then our decisions about who to spend time with change. Our actions with the people we do not want to spend time with change. Our actions don't change the abuser, but they change our social results. For example, we could avoid the abuser. It appears we now have the resolve not to be abused, but that is a consequence of all the deep work we did.

Motivate the Elephant

"Motivating the elephant" means discovering the things that will drive you and your team. According to Dan Pink, author of *Drive*, we need to pay attention to autonomy, mastery, and significance.[24] We are emotional creatures, and our limbic systems or emotional minds provide a high level of alertness to help motivate us. We are especially tuned in to the feelings of fear and love, which greatly impact the ways in which we operate.

When the elephant perceives it is being emotionally threatened, regardless of whether or not the threat is real, it will often react from the amygdala. This part of the brain is highly sensitive and has a memory for highly charged emotional events.[25] It is critical when attempting to motivate the elephant that we stick to elements and imagery that have a lasting emotive result. If a logical picture is essential for the rider, an emotional picture is needed for the elephant.

Shape the Path

The elephant is the most consistent predictor of behavior. Yet we often find ourselves mistreating the elephant in our blind desire to implement change in our lives.

The most likely path to maintaining resolve in achieving your goals is placing yourself in an environment that supports those goals. When most people think of shaping the path to success, they focus on their physical environments. That can definitely help, but it's not the whole picture. For instance, if you want to begin exercising regularly, you might begin to sleep in your gym clothes. If you want to save money, you might apply for a bank card that rounds up your change into a savings account.

The social environment, even more so than the physical environment, impacts an individual's resolve to achieve their goals. So, if you want to become more fit, hang around people who value that. If you want to read more, begin conversations with people who are growth oriented.

The Five P's of Vision

We want to claim victory in this battle of the rider and the elephant. The usual approach is to use the willpower of the rider to overpower the elephant. This is both foolish and dangerous since the rider is no match for the elephant's strength. To succeed, we need a strategy that uses the elephant and the rider for their strengths and mitigates their weaknesses.

Identified below are five traits that make up an effective vision. This vision will power our resolve and enable us to direct the rider, motivate the elephant, and shape the path.

Trait 1: A Powerful Vision

Emotion is your energy in motion. Nothing will motivate you if it doesn't capture your feelings. Every action you take is based upon a decision you made, coupled with emotional motivation. In many cases, people are under the impression that they are victims to circumstance, yet everything they do is based on a conscious or unconscious decision that is driven by an emotion. So, the picture you use to motivate yourself should bring out strong emotions in you.

Trait 2: A Personal Vision

When setting a goal or clarifying a vision, your behavior—and your behavior alone—must be the focus. This means that it is never about stopping other people's behavior as it relates to you. You—and you alone—must be the central figure in the picture frame.

Trait 3: A Present-Tense Vision

When I've assisted people in setting goals, this factor has often been the most difficult. We often categorize goals and dreams into a place called "there." We are plagued with destination disease; we assume our future vision will happen a long time from now or in a galaxy far, far away. Due to the futuristic nature of our hope, it never materializes because, categorically, the future is a place we are always headed but never quite reach. You should declare your goal in the present tense until it no longer feels disingenuous to say. Your goal must change from "I will be" to "I am."

Trait 4: A Positive Vision

Life can be convoluted with things that people dislike. Often, when people reflect on a preferred future, they instinctively think about all the things they don't want. They assume they will like their lives if they only get rid of all the things that annoy them.

Nothing could be further from the truth. For one, the mind does not understand negative expressions in a negative way. Instead, it understands the main idea and focuses on that. Whatever a person focuses on or gives their strongest energy to, whether it is couched in negative or positive terms, expands in their life.

This is why author Andy Stanley says it's a person's direction, not their intention, that determines their destination.[26] This truth is why highway patrol officers now go to a car's passenger side when pulling over drivers on the highway. Going to the driver's side led, unfortunately, to many people crashing into the officers. There was never any intention to crash into them, but as their focus went toward the flashing lights, drivers unwittingly drifted in the direction of their attention.

Likewise, when someone says they don't want to be poor, the mind creates all of its imagery based on poverty and not on the "don't."

As you can see, through our creative power, we build the world that entertains our focus. So, if you want something to occur in your life, focus on a positive picture of it.

Trait 5: A Pictorial Vision

The book of Proverbs in the Bible says, "Where there is no vision, people cast off restraint."[27] This means if you are not clear on your image, your ability to march confidently in the direction of your dreams is significantly reduced. To truly establish vision, we need an image that deeply resonates with what we are drawn to accomplish.

How Vision Creates Resolve

It is critical to have a strong vision in order to stay engaged. With a strong vision, you can form a detailed plan to attain your vision.

Making a plan does not guarantee success, but it calms the noise in the brain that causes us to abandon our dreams. Furthermore, it is unlikely that the first plan you make will be the final plan that succeeds. The first, second, and twentieth plans may all fail. We don't begin a plan because it is perfect. We begin a plan because it moves us in the direction we want to go.

The strength of our resolve is influenced and ultimately determined by many factors. In this chapter, we covered the strength of our desire to reach a goal, the context our goals exist within, the connection between character and goals, the battle between the rider and the elephant, and the strength of our vision.

We are all born with the same raw material, which is called time. One difference between the CEO and the disgruntled grocery store clerk is what they've done with their time. Use the knowledge you gained in this chapter to structure your time to pursue your goals.

PART II

BUILD EMOTIONAL STRENGTH TO WIN

THE BATTLE OF THE HEART

CAPITALIZE ON YOUR PASSION

CHAPTER 6

RELEASE

/rəˈlēs/

Allow or enable to escape from confinement; set free[1]

The best things to do with the best things
in life is to give them away.
—Dorothy Day[2]

In 2005, I moved to Costa Rica. Since I was not able to find tenants for my house in the United States before moving, I asked a friend if he could take charge and help me find tenants. I left with him the keys, the rental agreement, and bank account deposit slips for my rental house.

At the four-month point, I hadn't heard from my friend and hadn't seen any change in my bank account. I assumed my friend had been unsuccessful in renting out the house, but I was wrong. Over the Christmas holiday, I returned to check on things. When I talked to my friend, I discovered that he had given my keys away to a couple of his employees, and his employees had been living in my house for three months without paying a dime in rent.

I quickly went to the house. As I approached it, I couldn't help but notice a foul smell coming from the front door. As the couple opened the door, I was shocked to notice junk covering every inch of the house I could see. I literally could not see the floor. The house was a wreck.

When I talked to the couple to try to make sense of why they were living in my house rent-free, they were polite enough to point out to me that the toilet didn't work. It seemed that when they figured out weeks before that the toilet was broken, rather than calling a plumber, they simply kept using it. Most days, this couple and their four children drove to the gas station to use the restroom, but at night, they would often use the toilet in my home. Each flush caused the toilet to overflow, spilling onto the bathroom floor and spreading into the adjacent kitchen. That was why the house smelled disgusting.

Searching for the best solution to these multiple problems, I asked the couple if they would start paying rent if I solved the plumbing issue and got the house cleaned up. They said no and that if I was going to charge them rent, they were leaving.

After they left, I had to hire a professional cleaner to come in and clean the floors. The plumber I hired informed me that the oak tree outside had broken through the pipes and wouldn't allow anything through from the toilet. Between the cleaner and the plumber, it cost me more than four thousand dollars to clean up after the unwanted tenants left to make my house inhabitable once again.

The point I'm making is that the plumbing wasn't the only thing that had blocked these people's situation. As takers, they had stopped the flow of things, such as repairs, moving through their lives. They had "stinking thinking." They were willing to go to the length of driving to the gas station rather than having the toilet fixed. They depended on other people to solve their problems.

My unfortunate experience with the couple inhabiting my home paints a dark picture of people who do nothing but take. However, every extreme example has its opposite. At the opposite end of this spectrum of give-and-take are giving people. Giving people are a joy to be around because they are rivers of plenty and abundance. John Maxwell speaks to the idea of becoming giving people when he encourages us to become a river and not a reservoir.[3]

Takers display the worst part of humanity with their greed and selfishness. They will take your generosity and make it worthless. To avoid the consequences of a taking lifestyle, it is important we be givers and also disassociate ourselves from takers.

Control Issues

I've got control issues. Don't look at me like that—the fact is that you do too. But we are not born with control issues. As babies, we allow doctors, nurses, parents, and even jealous older siblings to change us, feed us, and give us shots without much resistance.

Fairly soon, we recognize that not all events are guaranteed to go the way we desire. We need to provide some resistance in order to influence events in our favor. The need to protect and defend ourselves from what Dr. Larry Crabb calls "soul wounds" that become inevitable:

> We have made a terrible mistake! For most of this century we have wrongly defined soul wounds as psychological disorders and delegated their treatment to trained specialists. Damaged psyches aren't the problem. The problem is disconnected souls.[4]

We all have experienced pain and challenges in life that have caused us to make motions to protect our souls.

We live in a broken society, and everyone at some point has been the recipient of damage that moves them toward self-protection. A highly sophisticated self-protection mechanism evolves as we learn ways to protect ourselves. This mechanism is unique to each person.

Pretty soon, our self-protection mechanism automatically turns on when we start the day. It affects how we approach and respond to situations. We don't want to leave ourselves vulnerable to the chance that someone might attack.

You might argue that a person can't be expected to live with their guard down. You may exclaim, "Only a fool would live with an open heart and open hand in such a dysfunctional society." The truth is that I have not perfected the discipline of living with complete openness and vulnerability—even among those I love the most. My own instincts have been shaped by self-protection.

However, there is a relationship between love and openness. This relationship suggests that the degree I am willing to be open is proportionate to the degree I am able to love. Author and theologian Greg Boyd says, "Love *is* a tremendous risk. But if humans ever concluded the risk was not worth it, we [would] likely become extinct rather quickly."[5]

The good we can do directly depends on our willingness to embrace the risk of being hurt. To do the greatest amount of good, we must be willing to risk the greatest amount of pain.

Consider the likes of Dr. Martin Luther King Jr., Mother Teresa, Mahatma Gandhi, Jesus Christ, and many other revolutionaries. They loved much, gave up control over their personal lives, and in many cases sacrificed themselves for the fulfillment of loving others. Without their openness and release of control, there would have been no movement and no progress. If you want to have a significant impact on the world, you must learn to let go of control.

The Giving Continuum

Whether it is in the plant, animal, or human world, there's a maturity continuum from taking to giving. The continuum starts with new life such as an infant, a bear cub, or a shrub sprout. These beginners have no capacity for giving or contributing. As a matter of survival, they need others, such as parents or a sustaining environment, to protect them until they are capable of providing for themselves. There is a graduation of sorts from youth to adult, from dependence to independence, where a life can at some level can survive without the need for others to provide and protect it.

Yet there is a higher level of living than independence; Stephen Covey referred to it as *interdependence*.[7] This is a state where, although we are capable of taking care of ourselves, we see the benefit of extending beyond ourselves. With a heart of gratitude, we contribute to others.

As Abraham Maslow suggested, we have to grow to understand that the highest levels of fulfillment are the commitments we make to actualizing our spiritual nature.[8] Our higher self experiences the joy and fulfillment of life but not through experiencing finer material goods. Joy and fulfillment happen through us expressing the elements of our higher nature, which are giving and being a blessing.

Unfortunately for many humans, when they are given the choice to mature and grow, they stay stuck. We should be grateful that plants don't elect to simply not grow and give back; talk about an immediate effect on our food supply. How about animals choosing not to protect their young or procreate? Our ecosystems would be in massive disarray.

I believe that many of the problems our world faces today, from war to natural disaster, are a reflection of many people—both in our generation and before—choosing not to live up to their potential and contribute to the world. We get tangled in webs trying to understand our own significance and build lives based on what others think about us. We seek to protect ourselves from ridicule or from the traps of the selfishness of others. The truth is, most of us don't give to our capacity because we are not certain what we think of ourselves.

Eric Hoffer, author of *The True Believer*, puts it this way:

> No matter what our achievements might be, we
> think well of ourselves only in rare moments. We

need people to bear witness against our inner judge, who keeps book on our shortcomings and transgressions. We need people to convince us that we are not as bad as we think we are.[9]

As we examine the maturity continuum, we see the lowest level of existence, which is to take and only take. Matching in human maturity is evidenced by people who both give and take—but only by reciprocating what happens to them. The next and final level, the giving level, is filled with those who primarily give.

We will examine the matching and giving phases later, but first we need to deal with an issue that is unique to human nature. We have an internal factor, unforgiveness, that blocks our flow and doesn't allow us to experience the abundance that comes from releasing. Let's look at forgiveness, which makes advancing from phase to phase possible.

Forgiveness

This story is difficult for me to write because it reflects an ugly part of my life. Committing it to print makes me feel extremely vulnerable. I hope the fact that this story is in the middle of the book means most people will skip over it. However, I am writing about it at all because I believe it will help someone and bring healing.

Most people who know me now don't believe it when I tell them I was a bit of a nerd growing up. I was a really good boy who, for the most part, followed all the rules. As the Christian faith was a major part of my life (and still is), I was not sexually active growing up. I was one of the rare teens who graduated from my high school still a virgin. In my faith community, I was treated like a really good kid: morally upright and spiritually strong. After high school, I chose to go to a small, private college in Minnesota that I felt reflected my values and my faith.

Two weeks into my first semester, I began to notice that I wasn't one of the coolest kids in school, but by my own estimation, I thought I should at least be somewhere in the middle of the cool rankings. I remember going to a party and hanging out with a girl I'm not sure if I was attracted to, but I was definitely enjoying her attention. We talked late into the night until there were just the two of us left, and the conversation turned really personal.

She began to share that she had left a home where she was sexually abused by her stepfather. She feared he would continue with her younger sister now that she was gone. I tried to be a good listener and was not really comfortable watching a girl cry, so when she asked if we could take a walk outside to get some fresh air, I thought nothing of it.

We walked through the park in the dark and stopped at the playground. I sat on the steps to the slide, and she leaned in to kiss me. I was feeling a lot of emotions because I had never heard a story like hers—and I had never kissed a white girl. I rejected her kiss, and her eyes got really big. She began to cry and ran toward the dorms. I followed her and tried to apologize because I wasn't exactly sure what had happened.

Two days later, I was called into the dean's office of this private school. The dean of students was contemplating throwing me out of school for breaking their strict rules. I couldn't figure out which rule I had broken. Then he mentioned the encounter I had in the park. I couldn't understand; I argued my case that she tried to kiss me. I asked how that put me in trouble. The dean informed me that school staff had interviewed sixteen people on each of the women's floors and heard from several women that they didn't think I was upholding the values of the school.

Later, a friend told me that the resident advisor (RA) on their floor asked their entire floor if anyone had had a bad experience with me. If they had, the RA said, they could come forward. I can't prove it, but I believe this was repeated on each floor. I was confronted by several young men who had cousins or sisters at the school. The young men sternly told me not to talk with their female relatives. My RA asked me if I had anything I wanted to pray about. For the life of me, I couldn't understand what was going on.

I grew up in Chicago on the South Side where firefighters, teachers, and police officers were the only white people we met. There were a few white students in my eighth grade class and at least a couple hundred in my high school, but I never really met any of them. We were taught racism was something that happened in the 1960s, and we actually were reminded of how we had overcome every Martin Luther King Jr. Day and the entire month of February (affectionately known as Black History Month). So, when one of the other black students at the college suggested that my treatment might be racially motivated, I vehemently denied it. I persisted in saying this was a huge misunderstanding.

In the end, I was not expelled. But after several incidents that demonstrated that I was not welcome at people's lunch tables, in common areas, or hanging out with certain people, I realized that I had been blackballed (no pun intended) by the student body.

I spent months thinking my voice was too loud, my jokes were misunderstood, and my hygiene was off. I was constantly changing things about myself to be accepted in that Bible college. Self-hatred grew in me for not being good enough.

I was mean to myself until, one day, I stopped. On that day, I walked into a dorm room to say hi to people I thought would be accepting because they were playing rap music, but they asked me to get out, saying they didn't like me. I went to my dorm room and cried. But then I had the insight that it wasn't me they didn't like because they didn't even know me. It came to me that the extreme investigation over a kiss, the bullying and threats to stay away from family members, the cold looks and moving away when I sat close by in the cafeteria were indeed racially motivated. That was the day I stopped my self-hate.

I was very hurt and broken by the treatment from the students and staff. As an eighteen-year-old kid, what could I do but quit school? I threw myself into two full-time jobs, got an apartment with friends who had moved to Minnesota from Chicago, and decided I didn't like white people.

I carried this weight around with me for more than two years until I heard a message on forgiveness at church. This message reminded me that no one who hurt me was thinking about me. I was the only person wounded and shaping my entire life around people who didn't care about me in the least. The pastor said unforgiveness is like drinking poison and waiting on someone else to die. It was hurting me and negatively shaping my future.

So, after church that day, I did something really crazy. I forgave them, every single one of them. I realized that no matter what they had done, it was not worth jading my life in a way that would jeopardize my future. So, I wept, slept, and woke up healed. This may sound incredible, but I felt such a love for people that I carry to this day. I went back to that school and passed my classes with flying colors. I showed love to some of the same people who had rejected me, knowing that their narrow perspective said more about them than it could ever say about me. This discovery that love is a choice forever marked my life.

I can truly say that I have compassion for people who are racist. I truly feel that they are blind to such a beautiful world. The beauty of living with an open heart is that you choose when you will close it, but you know that closing it does you more harm than good.

Daniel Goleman, the expert on emotional intelligence, suggests:

> Self-absorption in all its forms kills empathy, let alone compassion. When we focus on ourselves, our world contracts as our problems and preoccupations loom large. But when we focus on others, our world expands. Our own problems drift to the periphery of the mind and so seem smaller, and we increase our capacity for connection—or compassionate action.[10]

My capacity to connect increased once I forgave my fellow students and the college faculty. I released the pain of being hurt and stepped toward fulfilling my dreams. One of my dreams was to teach at that college after I graduated from it, which I did.

Takers, Matchers, Givers, Etcetera

The framing I've been using of takers, matchers, and givers comes from Adam Grant's book *Give and Take*.[11] Let's explore his definitions, their implications, and then a couple ideas of my own.

Takers

When you look at the lowest level of human existence, maturity consists of only taking what other people have—even to the point of stealing. (This is often a survival mechanism, whether the need for stealing is real or imagined.) Also, if a person sees themself as losing, they will feel the need to take.

When babies are born, their instincts are to focus only on things that will help them survive. Through extremely high, loud vocal pitches, they create a noise problem for anyone who is negligent in giving them what they need. They are unable to give during this phase, and their lives are centered around themselves. Children in the toddler phase of life will often fight for the right to take what they feel is theirs.

The longer a human being stays on the taking level, the more likely they are to repel other people. The adult who is stuck in a taking phase believes nice guys finish last. They believe in taking "them" for what "they're" worth. They justify their taking.

Most people who are considered takers find themselves taking in order to satisfy an inner emptiness of purpose. Takers can only momentarily experience happiness by taking and then must continue their quest for more to take. Those who only take ultimately find themselves dissatisfied and discouraged because they're trying to fill a void the wrong way.

When sailors go to sea, they are told never to drink the seawater if stranded because it will only give them momentary relief and will ultimately kill them. Staying in the taking phase too long is to the soul as drinking sea water is to the body—it may satisfy a short-term need, but it is eventually terminal.

There's another version of taking for humans that I'll call *withholding*. The withholder is not as needy as the taker, but they are still holding back what they're capable of giving. Withholding occurs when people feel the need to protect themselves from being harmed. At the same time, they're not allowing themselves to be conduits of generosity.

Withholding demonstrates a person's inability to live up to their potential. Releasing love or power or those things that will add value to other people is central to what it means to be living out our potential. The withholder also lacks energy to live life because it takes a lot of energy to withhold. People who are withholding are holding in good energy along with the bad.

If takers don't release their negative emotions in appropriate ways, their negative emotions become toxic and do damage. Those people who are just takers often spew the negative energy of hate and violence.

Matchers

Matchers are essentially locked into a world where they don't want to offset the balances; they want everything to be fair. They want to make sure they don't give too much or take too much. They have pure motives, and their approach feels fair in the short term, but this constant balancing turns into an energy drain.

Underneath, matchers are living out of fear that someone is going to be taken advantage of, whether it be them or someone else. Matchers work extremely hard to make sure they don't take advantage of people and they're not being taken advantage of. But when they have to monitor things with such vigilance, they lose the meaning of the word "generosity."

When matchers don't release their negative emotions in appropriate ways, these emotions become toxic and do damage. Turned inward, their negative emotions become anxiety. Turned outward, they become manipulation, rants, or violence.

Givers

Givers are people who are on the generosity end of the give-take maturity continuum. The least giving of givers gives unconditionally to those they love. There's a middle group who give unconditionally to those they love and also to acquaintances. Then there's the far end of the continuum, populated by people who give unconditionally to those they love, to acquaintances, and to strangers. These people are truly generous; they are people who add value to the world.

From the outside, it often looks as if takers have more than givers, and so it seems that takers would be more satisfied than givers. But, through many forms of research, it has been proven that those who give have happier lives.[13]

At a young age, a person learns how to act within society and what role they will play. They learn the rules and expectations of society's unwritten social contract. They learn if they're only a taker, the social environment will reject them and shame them for not sharing, while if they're only a giver, they will be considered a pushover and will be taken advantage of. There are expectations depending on the environment they find themselves in. As a businessperson, you are expected to be more of a shark; at a nonprofit organization, you are expected to be more of a bleeding heart.

We mature into the expectations of the social contract of our culture. Givers receive social acceptance, and takers are often socially rejected. Relationships are formed out of acceptance, and dissonance is created out of rejection. Over time, we learn our roles and create beliefs around them.

But what happens when the social contract contradicts our internal impulse to keep? The internal voice says, "If I share, I don't have." Instinctively, we have a scarcity mindset, a fear of losing things, while externally, there's a social pressure that's trying to extract from us, asking us to share things. We wrestle with that tension.

The irony is that if we do the opposite of our instinct to keep, we will be rewarded internally. In addition to receiving external social rewards, people who freely give experience feelings of internal freedom.

Now, the construction of this argument isn't to pit takers against givers. However, some givers (designated by Grant as "otherish givers") end up having more satisfaction and happiness, and they also accumulate more successes and more financial wealth than matchers and takers.

Of all three identities, givers have the easiest time releasing their emotions in appropriate ways. Givers are already releasing their wealth the way people are supposed to; releasing their emotions naturally follows. Gretchen Rubin, the author of *The Happiness Project*, says givers must be strong:

> The belief that unhappiness is selfless and happiness is selfish is misguided. It's more selfless to act happy. It takes energy, generosity, and discipline to be unfailingly lighthearted, yet everyone takes the happy person for granted. No one is careful of his feelings or tries to keep his spirits high. He seems self-sufficient; he becomes a cushion for others. And because happiness seems unforced, that person usually gets no credit.[14]

Giving Unconditionally

Giving does not mean being a doormat or giving without self-consideration. But consider the impact of giving unconditionally when you give without the expectation of anything being returned to you. When you give with the expectation of something being returned, it's possible to become angry, hostile, and bitter when the receiver doesn't reciprocate. But those who give freely, with no expectation of a return, are in a much better position, a stronger position because they won't be disappointed.

That reminds me of a time I asked a college friend for some money. He would not give it to me, even though he had the money at the time. When I pressed him as to why he would not give it to me, he said it was because he'd learned to only give what he was willing to walk away from. Then, if the money was never returned, he wouldn't harbor any negative feelings.

He said he couldn't give the money to me without expectation because, although he had the money at the moment, he would need it later. If I didn't pay it back in time, it would create tension in the relationship, and our relationship was too important to him for that to happen. I thought that demonstrated a profound level of self-awareness.

Receiving from Equals

Releasing is ultimately an issue of control. I learned this when I moved to Minnesota.

When I graduated from college and started my career in the nonprofit world, I needed volunteers. My university was close to where I worked, and I thought it was the best place I could recruit these volunteers. The college kids I recruited came cheap. All they needed from me was free pizza once a month. One night when I was dropping them off back at their school, I decided to pick up a late-night meal for them at a chicken shack. The neighborhood the chicken shack was in was a little suspicious, so we decided to go back to the school to eat the meal. We set up our food in one of the common areas. It was apparent I was from a big family because although there were only six of us, I had ordered enough for ten.

We talked, and the conversation turned to etiquette. I revealed to them my theory of three yeses. I said that since I moved to Minnesota, I had noticed a cultural difference from what I was used to back in Chicago. I noticed that in Minnesota, if I wanted to offer someone food, I had to offer it three times for them to accept it. The unspoken protocol in Minnesota is that the first time someone offers food, the potential receiver always says no. At that point, if the person is truly offering and not simply doing the polite thing, they ask a second time, "Would you like some food?" The respondent says one of two things: 1) If they want to refuse, they say, "No, thank you. I just ate." 2) Or if the respondent actually wants the food, they say something like, "No, thank you. That's yours." Then the giver says, "It's okay. I won't be able to eat it all." Only then does the receiver accept the food.

To me, this seemed like a lot of mental gymnastics to go through for a bite of food, but after finding myself on the wrong side of the equation too many times, I learned. A couple of times as the giver, I asked only once and watched in dismay as the hungry potential receiver, who only meant to give me a polite no, felt too ashamed to ask for the food. Other times, as a potential receiver, I had foolishly said yes to the giver's first offer. They had expected me to say "No, thank you," but I didn't and so was quickly deemed rude.

Within minutes of explaining my theory to my wonderful volunteers, we had a chance to see it in action. A poor college student sat down and simply gave me the "I'm hungry but too ashamed to ask for anything" look. I offered her some pizza, and the conversation played out exactly the way I had said it would. The entire table of volunteers spent the next few hours laughing uncontrollably.

The point is, receiving when in need may take humility, but a person's pride is overcome by need. Receiving when entitled takes no amount of grace whatsoever. However, receiving from an equal position, especially when the gift is not needed, takes strength and security. This includes receiving material gifts, compliments, and recognition. In most cases, because of pride, it is more difficult to receive than it is to give. The ultimate in emotional security is when a giver (a person who is whole enough not to be a taker) can be a receiver.

> Until we can receive with an open heart, we're never really giving with an open heart. When we attach judgment to receiving help, we knowingly or unknowingly attach judgment to giving help.
> —Brené Brown[15]

Stuck Stinks

In Greek mythology, there was a young hunter who was known for his beauty. Everywhere he went, many adored him and loved him for his beauty, yet he showed nothing but contempt and disdain for these people. He found no one worthy of him.

One day, the young hunter met Echo, a nymph. Echo made a romantic advance toward him, but he rejected her. Nemesis, the goddess of retribution and revenge, became annoyed and caused the hunter to see his reflection in a pool of water. Immediately, he thought he had found someone worthy of his love. Yet he discovered that it was a love he could never possess, as it was merely his own reflection. This caused him to fall into a great despair and eventually a depression that left him with no choice but to die by that pool.

The young hunter's name was Narcissus, and it is from his name that we get our term *narcissism*. So, you can see, even the ancient Greeks, who justified self-love in many of their practices, knew the dangers of complete narcissism. Narcissism is contrary to releasing and giving. It is about holding on to. It is about not sharing.

This chapter covered the opposite of narcissism—what it means to give, "to release." We looked at giving up control to love more deeply, the giving continuum, forgiveness, takers, matchers, givers, unconditional giving, and receiving.

A final thought as we close this chapter comes from Friedrich Nietzsche: "This is the hardest of all: to close the open hand out of love, and keep modest as a giver."[16]

CHAPTER 7

RECREATE

/ˌrēkrēˈāt/

Create again[1]

Attitude is a choice. Happiness is a choice. Optimism is a
choice. Kindness is a choice. Giving is a choice. Respect is a
choice. Whatever choice you make makes you. Choose wisely.
—**Roy T. Bennett**[2]

One of the curses of being a visionary leader is that there is no end
to the amount of stress you can create in your life. Case in point, as
a director of a nonprofit, I used to throw a leadership conference for
emerging leaders. If you've ever thrown a conference, you are already
holding your breath as you read this because you know the amount
of work that goes into it.

For my nonprofit event, multiply that stress by ten because all
the volunteers and staff were occupied with putting out a million
day-to-day fires within the organization, so they couldn't help
me. To be fair, my nonprofit staff and volunteers were all there for

the brainstorming meeting. Some came for the free Little Caesars pizza. Others came because they loved the dreaming part, but not so much the work part. Either way, come execution time, it fell on me to tie up all the loose ends and, with the help of a small committee, make goody bags for the hundreds of participants in the hotel.

After months of promotion, working seventy-plus hours a week for at least twelve weeks in a row, selling tickets, marketing to several audiences, and preparing for the speakers coming to town, I was stressed. The work was nonstop. On top of everything, the keynote presenter was someone I really looked up to. So, although each event was important, I put extra pressure on myself for this event to live up to the expectations I was sure the keynote speaker had of my organization.

To be honest, this weekend was not unique for me. It simply exposed the pattern of behavior I had: being addicted to the adrenaline rush I got from living in a performance-based, stress-filled world. I was twenty-seven years old and growing gray hairs by the moment as I worked myself from event to event in order to make a positive impact on people's lives. Three days prior to this event, we had finally sold out the conference space, and that should have been the ultimate success. But that was not good enough for me.

I felt I had to be the master of ceremonies because the transitions needed to be perfect. I felt I had to exuberantly greet people at the registration table because I didn't trust the volunteers to have enough positive energy to greet the participants. I even felt I had to provide transportation for the speakers because we certainly couldn't risk them having a bad experience at the airport if one of the volunteers forgot their gate number or where to park.

I needed to make sure that the event went perfectly because if it didn't, it might reflect negatively on our ability to host events in the future. I treated every task as urgent, everything as mission critical. It was clear to anyone viewing things from the outside that I was high-strung. Yet as easy as it may be to criticize, I assure you that from where I was sitting, everything I did had a reason, and all of my micromanagement was justified.

That is, until I went to pick up the keynote speaker. I remember picking him up from the airport and driving him to the hotel. I was polite and full of flattery for the first few moments, but my driving was hurried and a bit erratic. He easily picked up on my frazzled demeanor, but rather than interrupt my unbreakable steam train, he made small talk. He asked questions about the event, the audience, and what he could expect as far as arrangements back to the airport after he was done.

I was completely unaware that he was observing me and patiently waiting for the perfect moment to confront me about the fact that I was neglecting myself, my health, and my closest relationships in the name of the noble ambition to do good. As I politely carried his baggage to his hotel room, he paused and asked me what I was about to do. I really didn't want to go down my entire to-do list, but I smiled. Honestly, though, I was a little annoyed by the question because I believed he wanted to interrupt my unquenchable drive to host a successful event.

In order to ensure I didn't demonstrate a lack of confidence in the event, I told him that I was just going to wrap up some last-minute things. Truthfully, on the inside, I was a busy and nervous wreck and felt I needed to do something, anything, but make small talk. My guest persisted in assuming there was nothing really important that I had to do and told me to go get my swim trunks and head with him down to the pool, where he had some important things to share with me. When I mentioned I didn't have any trunks, he politely said, "No worries. I'll loan you a pair."

I was really frustrated and tried pushing back. I told him I appreciated the gesture, but I had things to get done because there was no one else who was going to do the menial tasks.

He said, "I won't take no for an answer. I insist you join me."

My annoyance simmered into a visible frustration, which he simply ignored. He grabbed some *Time* and *Sports Illustrated* magazines that appeared to be at least a decade old. These magazines had pictures of historical sports and political figures, but very few words. What did he want with old magazines?

I asked my guest if he wouldn't mind if I jumped in the pool and swam a few laps—I wanted to get in a workout to feel at least a little productive.

Instead, he said, "No, join me in the hot tub," in a way only a mentor whom you respect could dictate.

As we went into the hot tub, he handed me a copy of *Time* that walked through the 1960s. He told me to look through the pictures, but not to read the articles—just look at the photos and, most importantly, not think about anything I had to do for the rest of the day. I was secretly thinking, *I thought you had something important to discuss. This is stupid and a complete waste of time.*

For the first few minutes, I couldn't stop thinking about the things that weren't being done, but I soon noticed the calmness of the environment, the serenity on the faces in the photos, and the peaceful feeling of being in warm water. After twenty minutes of not talking, thinking, or worrying, my entire demeanor was different, and finally my guest began to talk.

My mentor taught me one of the most important lessons of my life in less than half an hour. He taught me that no one will benefit from all I have to offer if I diminish my value by performing at a level where I show only a fragment of my true potential.

How Creating, Recreation, and Recreating Relate to Each Other

In other words, my mentor taught me that my ability to continuously create hinges on my ability to recreate myself and my ability to recreate myself hinges on me taking time for recreation.

"All achievements, all earned riches, have their beginning in an idea," wrote Napoleon Hill.[3] These ideas often become tired, exhausted, burned-out, and frustrated because of the complexity of life and our propensity to overthink. We don't set aside time to rejuvenate our thinking; instead, we find ourselves on an increasingly busy treadmill and becoming more and more dull. Does this sound like you sometimes?

Then there is this problem. Most ideas that have incredible potential are actually stillborn: they die before they even get the opportunity to live. This often happens because we share these ideas with people who tear them down or rip them apart. Either they discourage us—or we allow our own inner voices to discourage ourselves from actually putting these thoughts, these creative ideas, on the drawing boards of our minds to see what's possible.

The one way in which we can almost certainly guarantee the protection of these ideas, not only to survive but to grow and thrive, is through the process of *create, recreation, recreate*. When we allow our creative energy to be renewed, restored, and developed, we can release creative thoughts on a new plane.

It must be intentional that the word *recreation* is born of the word *creation*. Literally, *recreation* means to create again. From the massive complexity of unfocused recreation come focused, new ideas.

Unfocused sunshine is extremely powerful, yet people can stand outside for hours and only get a tan. A laser is weak by comparison, but as it is focused, it can burn holes in some of the hardest substances on Earth. You can be unfocused and marginally effective or focused and highly effective. If we are unfocused and undisciplined in our thinking, we will be driven by every stress and strain that pulls us in a hundred different directions. Success requires the power of focused thought.

Critical achievement, as Napoleon Hill pointed out, begins with an idea. The time in which those ideas germinate, incubate, and launch has to be protected and preserved. Recreation time has to be preserved so we can regenerate ourselves with enough energy for the creative aspects of our internal genius to be released.

We Are Born to Create

That happens because we show others that it is safe to be liberated from fear. People are inspired by and aspire to be like the people who shine the light, who express their creativity in our society.

We Are Born for Recreation

As I learned from my mentor, recreation gives us the ability to relax, recharge, and operate at our optimum level. We don't think of a prison term as a time of recreation, but it is a time away from the busyness of everyday affairs. Down through the ages, think of what has been written in the seclusion of prison cells. For example, imprisoned apostles wrote many books of the New Testament. John Bunyan wrote the classic *Pilgrim's Progress* while he was incarcerated. Dr. Martin Luther King Jr. wrote his "I Have a Dream" speech, for the most part, in a prison cell. Time away from the usual activities is important for creating and recreating.

If we live with no margins—that is, with no boundaries of time and space for our activities—we may not set aside the creative thinking time needed to reach our goals. John Maxwell calls this "planned neglect," which is where we choose to not do certain things in order to create time for what's important for reaching our goals. I suggest we apply planned neglect to make live dreaming and recreation a priority.[5]

As we creative beings think, our thoughts naturally create our future, for good or for bad. James Allen was famous for saying, "The soul attracts that which it secretly harbors; that which it loves, and also that which it fears."[6] Our thought impulses are either forging for us weapons by which we destroy ourselves or creating heavenly mansions of joy and peace.

Because control of our creative faculties is compromised with mental and physical fatigue, we have one option if we are to grow and expand. That option is recreation so we can have energy to recreate.

The difference between those of us who create the lives we want and those of us who create lives we want to escape from is the degree of control we have over our minds. To paraphrase Thomas Troward, as spiritual beings, we cannot divest ourselves of the inheritance to create; it is part of our creative imagination.[7] Yet, if we want to direct our minds to create what we desire, we must discipline the mind to allow it to create a positive space for our desires to flourish.

That positive space is carved out through recreation. It seems contradictory to discipline our minds to take time for recreation, but that is what we need to do.

We Are Born to Recreate

Our primitive instinct draws us constantly into the negative of life, and this exhausts our spirits and wears us out. We do this because out of our two primal motives of fear and love, fear is the stronger impulse. We fear and our thoughts turn negative.

Fear can send us into regretting and fretting. Remember I mentioned "regretting and fretting" in chapter 3? If we want an amazing future, we must pay close attention to the direction of our thinking. We must think positive thoughts about our future. We all must. Recreating the human experience is the responsibility of us all.

I'll revisit here the importance of protecting our energy if we want to recreate our lives and experience the true fruitfulness and abundance of life. Supporting this idea is the fact that many will spend all their health to obtain their wealth and then must spend all their wealth in an attempt to regain good health. The impact of stress-related disorders in our society, as well as mental illnesses, should be enough to get our attention. Humans must realize that activity is not equal to progress and that a high quantity of work can significantly limit its quality. An inability to rest, recover, and recreate makes our lives less than they could be.

The science-fiction film *The Matrix* is about a human computer hacker, Neo, who joins forces with human rebels to defeat aliens. There is a scene in the film when the main character, Neo, the "One," realizes his full potential. He decides to not be a victim of or subject to the rules of the Matrix anymore. Because of that decision, he effortlessly dismantles the attacks of his alien nemesis, "Smith." Neo's presence of mind allows him to understand the law of cause and effect in the Matrix, and that empowers him to operate at a higher level.[9]

I make no claims that your ability to recreate—your ability to bring about a rebirth of your creativity—will allow you to reinvent the laws of physics like Neo, but I can assure you that you are much more powerful than you realize. Your fully realized potential will cause you to gasp. All of us have the power to recreate our worlds.

In *The Hidden Power,* Thomas Troward explains:

> At every moment we are dealing with an infinitely sensitive medium which stirs creative energies that give form to the slightest of our thought-vibrations. This power is inherent in us because of our spiritual nature, and we cannot divest ourselves of it ... If it is not used to build up, it will destroy.[10]

Let's not destroy. Let's make the world a better place through our creating, recreation, and recreating.

Our Physical Bodies Support Recreating

As human beings, we are made up of more than fifty trillion cells, and each cell has all the systems we have as humans. It is amazing to discover that each of your cells is a mini-you. Each cell contains the functions of an epidermis or skin, a digestive, reproductive, respiratory, excretory, musculoskeletal, endocrine, nervous and immune system.[11] Your cells replace themselves year after year. You may already know this: almost every year, you are physically an entirely new person.

It is remarkable that our regenerating cells communicate so well with one another that they can pass down diseases for generations. Epigenetics, the study of what affects our genes, is discovering ways to realign the messaging within the cells by changing the messages cells pass down to new cells.[12] Many of these discoveries about how our cells operate support the process of self-recreation that I am proposing in this chapter.

Godlike in Three Ways

In the book of Genesis in the Bible, we see God creating, organizing, and delegating. He created the ocean, land, air, plants, and animals. He organized them by arranging each in a place. He delegated responsibility for Earth and its creatures to us humans.

In the Hebrew tradition, the word for spirit is *Ruach*, or "to breathe."[13] In the creation story given in the Torah, God breathed spirit into a human, which was distinct from speaking into being the rest of creation, including the stars, planets, and vast galaxies. After twenty-five verses of creating the universe, God then mentions that he created humans in his image and after His likeness and gave them power to rule.

We are godlike in that we, too, can create, organize, and delegate. When we create, we give from the spirit within us; we are inspired. The word *inspiration* comes from the Latin word *inspire*, which means to breathe.[14] Inspiration emerges from our spirit, and once we give our visions life, they breathe and bring out more life. The spirit is, in essence, who we are; it is the conscious self. The spirit reflects our true nature and gives us purpose, meaning, and significance.

The spirit creates things as magnificent as space shuttles to orbit and explore the vastness of our universe. That same spirit can also create a world of war, poverty, and disease. The outcome depends on what we submit our highest ambitions or our most destructive tendencies to.

I believe a truly spiritual person has the power to shape and change their environment, including their future. This is our unique, God-given endowment.

You Are Creative

We have to be cautious when we use the word *creation* because not all thought leaders agree on its definition. Creation assumes that a thing born from a human being's imagination didn't exist prior to its invention. In *The Creative Process in the Individual*, Troward suggests that all things in the universe are of the same substance, which he refers to as God.[15] Some people refer to it as energy or life force, others as chi, and Wallace D. Wattles describes it as "formless stuff."[16]

No matter how you refer to it, if it is true that we are not bringing things into existence but tapping into the unfolding or revealing of that which was hidden, we can abandon the myth that some people are creative and others are not. We can all seek creativity, knock on its door, and see it open. Even the least ingenious person can search for a mystery and focus on it long enough to find its answer.

My company, Experience Leadership Coaching & Training, is committed to exploring the limits of human potential. We discover business leaders every day who are unknowingly suppressing the potential buried within them. We are not creating potential; we are releasing it within our business clients.

Embrace Your Childlike Curiosity

Our thoughts are impulses and vibrations that are always creating. As babies, we are naturally creative and resourceful because there is no cognitive filter. We are actively making meaning out of images because meaning does not yet exist for them within us. In other words, babies don't have labels or categories for the physical world they experience. Children from infancy through the toddler years are thinking about what they see and actively creating meaning.

A drive to learn and grow puts that knowledge into a child's mind. For a child, a stick becomes a music-making machine, and facial hair becomes a nice pull toy. To a toddler, everything must be tasted, and for a three-year-old boy, almost everything, no matter how benign, becomes a weapon of some sort. A child's creative genius sees things that those of us who have stopped asking questions can't even dream of seeing. A child's insatiable curiosity enables them to see multiple meanings within the world and create fantasies to associate with their newfound knowledge.

Adults get frustrated and try to teach children to settle for the easy answer. We don't have the patience to constantly answer question after question. We know that the more questions we answer, the deeper the natural curiosity of the child will become. Over time, our brains become predictive machines and begin to create concrete meaning out of the world around us. In part, this happens because our pattern recognition mechanisms make associations with the outside world to reduce the enormous flow of information that comes in.

The impact is that children learn to stop asking questions and thus squelch their curiosity because primitive social sensitivities for acceptance override their need to know. Finally, around the age of six, as our cognitive filters attempt to eliminate things that seem irrelevant, our reticular activating systems bring to our conscious minds only the information that they deem relevant.

When children turn six, we begin to hear them say they are bored. That is an indication that they are losing their curiosity. This stage demonstrates that humans build up a resistance to chasing new information. This resistance limits our learning and minimizes the power of a self-improving mind.

The self-improving mind displays *neuroplasticity*, which is the ability of neural networks in the brain to change through growth and reorganization. These changes range from individual neurons making new connections to systemic adjustments like cortical remapping. For instance, cortical remapping occurs after an amputation—the old connections in the brain don't apply anymore, and so the brain reorganizes.[17]

For adults, there are things that tend to trigger our curiosity, but we have limits to expediency on how far we will allow curiosity to drive us. Many people deny being creative because they evaluate creativity based on a finished product and not an open-ended question. Since they don't have evidence of becoming masters at a skill, they think they are not creative.

Michelangelo worked on forty-six different statues, but only twenty-two were ever finished—and only one is still talked about. People consider him one of the greatest artists who ever lived, but had he never finished even one, it would not have diminished the amount of curiosity and creativity in his approach to life.

We get into a comparison game. Something internally has taught us that if we can't be the best in class, then we ought not try. We have this fixed mindset where we've defined our ability through comparison. And so, for example, some people will say, "I can't draw." They say they can't do this or that, and they resign themselves to a life of watching other people create. They never put in the effort, and their words become a self-fulfilling prophecy.

If there is one trait we all need that children possess in abundance: the curiosity born of recreation. Recreation relaxes our minds from needing to know all the answers and empowers us to become curious again.

Final Thoughts

You don't get a choice; you are going to create your life. Your life is a reflection of what you consistently create on the drawing board of your mind. Most of us lack the power to control our thoughts. Some people may be thinking, *If my thoughts determine my life, and I can't fully control my thoughts, then it's settled. I'm not in control. Therefore, I might as well go with the flow.*

Not so fast! There is hope if we embrace the journey of transformation. At the same time, we must resist the urge to give in to lower desires and competing beliefs—even if those desires and beliefs war against the preferred future we are seeking. Take the following four action steps in order to bring yourself the recreation your heart needs to achieve every dream you have:

Action Step 1

Take a vacation, a weekend, or a silent retreat in order to create a personal vision for yourself. This cannot happen in the middle of a hurried day. To recreate yourself, you must first create space. Reaching back to chapter 5, we will use the same requirements to supply energy to this image. Remember, since we behave from the dominant pictures in our mind, we must cultivate imagery that is visual, positive, emotional, present tense, and personal. Once you are clear on the vision, go to Action Step 2.

Action Step 2

Set up structures to control the flow of information that you take in. Write priorities on an index card that support your vision. For thirty days, surround yourself with time, space, and information that will allow you to remind yourself daily of what is important to you. Create structures that will support your priorities. Learn to hold on to your vision in this tangible way. If you want to go deeper, see what positive confessions you need to make to yourself in order to eradicate the negative voices.

Action Step 3

Create daily and weekly moments of recreation. It's not what we can do in one day that changes us; it's what we do daily over time. Like with anyone who wants to be a professional, practice is essential. We must create deliberate practices of prayer and meditation and reflect on what's important. If you don't have daily practices, I recommend starting with *The Miracle Morning* by Hal Elrod.[18]

Action Step 4

Find a person or a less fortunate group than you and come up with ways to serve them. This is how we can exercise our spiritual muscles that put us in touch with the eternal. A time of refreshing by serving others envelops us and gives us energy.

In this chapter, we looked at how creating, recreation, and recreating affect our future. We challenged the idea of working continuously and pointed out the need for recreation. I shared action steps you can take to improve your creative resilience.

CHAPTER 8

REJOICE

/rəˈjois/

To feel or show great joy or delight[1]

It is better to lead from behind and to put others in front, especially when you celebrate victory when nice things occur. You take the front line when there is danger. Then people will appreciate your leadership.
—Nelson Mandela[2]

Who is the happiest person you know? As you think through the different people and faces, I am certain there is one common denominator for them all. The happiest person you know does not have an easier or better life than anyone else you know; they simply choose to be content with whatever life brings them.

This idea occurred to me when I was working at a nonprofit a few years back. Many times, we would bring college student leaders in to work in an impoverished neighborhood with other nonprofits. One year, a young lady from a private university came to help us. We'll call her Emily.

On a Saturday morning, Emily assisted us in separating clothing and household items for families. We spent about four and a half hours unpacking and separating donated boxes of toys, clothes, dishes, and just about anything you could think of.

At exactly 1:00 p.m., the doors to the building burst open with dozens of people coming in to shop for clothes, toys, etc. Many of the people acted like kids in a candy store (in a toy store was more like it).

Emily successfully helped families here and there. Then, suddenly, as she was helping a family find shoes for the children, she left them, ran to the back room, and burst into tears. She cried loudly and was almost inconsolable. I walked back to check on her; I'm sure the people there were confused and wondered what was wrong with her. When I handed her some water, she calmed down a bit and got her breathing under control.

I asked her what had happened to cause such an emotional outburst. I asked if someone had said or done anything that triggered a horrible memory. "No," she replied. "It's so sad that those families don't have enough money to buy their own clothes—that they have to come here and get handouts."

I'm not sure why, but I asked her to tell me about her family. She began to share with me that she was one of two siblings who lived in a wealthy suburb of Minneapolis. She lived with her mom and stepdad, and her brother lived with their dad and stepmom. The siblings had lived together with their mom after the divorce, but after their mom met the man who would become her new husband, Emily's brother began to act unruly, scored poor grades in school, and began experimenting with drugs.

A blame game commenced. Emily's mom blamed her son's behavior on her ex-husband leaving to be with another woman. Emily's dad blamed Emily's mom and her new husband's bad parenting. Eventually, the mom grew weary of being blamed and wanted to prove the dad wrong—so she ordered him to come pick up his son.

After hearing her tearstained story, I invited her to look through the window to where families were shopping. I said, "Something is truly wrong when you feel sorry for these families who have each other, but you come from a broken home. These people don't have much money, but they have no stigma about wearing clothes or playing with toys that others no longer need. In many cases, the parents are immigrants and are proud to live in a country of abundance and generosity."

I wanted her to realize that poverty, like abundance, is not an income level but a condition of the heart. These financially poor families were rich in love, family, and ambition. The scene made me feel confident in the spirit of America, which takes in immigrants with dreams and makes them into entrepreneurs.

Emily continued to grieve for the families, but I hope her day with us planted a seed for personal growth.

Never Enough

There is a connection between joy and contentment that also exists between misery and greed. Those who are joyful are not typically wealthier. In fact, the happiest country in the world is not the wealthiest one.[3, 4, 5]

Zig Ziglar said, "Money won't make you happy, but everybody wants to find out for themselves."[6] This is true, but it is unfortunate that so many people trade happiness that they could easily secure by living within a budget. Instead, they live in misery by chasing a status they may never attain.

The human appetite is insatiable when it does not learn contentment. Stephen Covey suggests that contentment is obtained by balancing production and production capability.[7] If we have nothing, we are sure to be dissatisfied, but if we have something with no capacity to get more, we may spend our lives defending what we have. We have abundance when we have what we are after *and* the ability to achieve more.

Covey then connects this principle to Aesop's fable of the goose and the golden egg. Here's the story. A down-on-his-luck farmer comes home to find that his beloved goose has laid a golden egg. This happens daily, and the man becomes rich. He eventually becomes so greedy that he wants all the golden eggs at once, so he kills the goose, only to reach inside her body and find nothing. In the name of more production, he killed production capability.

If we are going to rejoice, which is the act of rejoining the chorus of the joyful, we must first define what we are after. It may seem strange, but I have seen the radiant joy of life more on the faces of the poor than I have seen on those who have great means.

When I think of joy, I don't see a wealthy palace. I think of the face of a squatter in Guatemala City in Zona 18 when I invited him to play soccer with me. I also think of the look on the face of a young, proud husband in Hyderabad when he received word that he had been accepted into a farming school.

I think of my grandmother, Eleanor, whom I never heard complain about anything. My grandmother's joy may not mean much to you. If not, you can move on, but I penned a letter to her a few years ago about the impact her positive attitude had on my life, and I want to give you insight into her joyful character by sharing the letter with you.

But first, let me describe my grandmother. She stood four feet eleven inches at her tallest, but she was tall and mighty as a follower of Jesus her whole life. Her husband, my grandfather, was a controversial African American pastor during the 1950s, '60s, and '70s. He was not afraid to call out political figures and government officials about injustices on his radio show "The Midnight Credo of Righteousness." Because of his fiery nature, he received death threats that came to their house through the mail and over the phone.

My grandmother did not want her eight children to live in fear, and she also wanted to set a tone for these phone calls, so she answered every call with a cheerful "Praise the Lord!" We grandchildren didn't even know about our grandfather's political activity and the threatening phone calls and mail until years later. My grandmother lived her faith, and that's why I want to share this letter with you.

Grandma,

I want to say thank you and that I thank God for you. I want to acknowledge you have been a source of encouragement in my life. I am not sure why it took me so long to see it. In the past year, I have been able to travel all over the North and Latin American continents, and now find myself in Costa Rica.

I have always had your support in both prayer and finances. I know that much of the family pulls on you for support and recently has looked for ways to repay you. I feel it's my place to share with you that through us, your children and grandchildren, your legacy will live on for many generations.

I bought a phone so that I can call the United States, but as of today, it still has not come. I am beginning to think that I will be back in the United States for Christmas before it gets here.

Since I have been here, I've been amazed at how much I have thought of you and Granddaddy during my prayer times. I think of you especially when I think of launching into the next phase of ministry. It is scary for me to launch into the next phase. Maybe you felt the same way when you moved to Chicago.

I am learning Spanish, but I don't have many people to speak with, so in the evenings I have been reflecting on who I am today. I am encouraged by your many stories I have heard over the years—from the days of fasting for Uncle Caesar's miraculous recovery as a child, the car slipping off the mountain in North Carolina, and, even more recently, the sustaining of your life without surgery. I remember six days of church services a week and three church services on Sunday. I remember all-night prayer vigils and hearing your affirmation for staying all night.

You have forever marked my life in ways that I cannot express with words. Only that Great Day will reveal all that you have done for and meant to people, especially me, in this life. I hope we will get many more years to appreciate you and receive your encouragement.

I have to share this story with you. That last time I visited you was while you had hurt your leg. As a reflective person, I am always searching to see if life principles are being lived out.

When I was visiting you, I was studying the connection between gratitude and emotional health. As you already know, we live in a very sick society. One sign of a sick society is when the medical terms that describe sicknesses become common household language. Our society is suffering so much from antisocial behavior that we nonmedical personnel have become very familiar with medical terms such as attention deficit hyperactive disorder (ADD and ADHD), multiple personality disorder, and schizophrenia.

It scares me that our solution for antisocial behavior is not socialization, but medication. One book I read suggested that what makes us so stressed as a society is our preoccupation with self and selfish behavior. The author suggested that if we would only stop to appreciate God's gifts, we would be less likely to be so consumed with self and less likely to have social disorders.

So, I was looking for cases where gratitude produces joy. And when I visited you, how wonderful it was to hear how many times you verbally gave thanks. When I was at your house, you were sitting with your foot propped up and you were a little under the weather, but you gave God praise at least once for every minute I was there. Even after you mentioned that you were in pain, you thanked God by saying, "He is faithful."

You blessed me that day because I know that in a world of skeptics, you testify to the power of a grateful heart. How much healthier we would be if we would only stop to be thankful. You remind me of another Eleanor (Roosevelt) who said, "Happiness is not a goal ... it's a by-product of a life well lived."

I love you, Grandma, and thank you for all you have done and continue to do.

Your grandson,
Stephen

Your Heart, Your Choice

In *The Life You've Always Wanted*, John Ortberg shares an experience from one of his friends, Tom Schmidt.[8] Reading Tom's story left me speechless.

John recounts Tom's experience at a state-run hospice. At the home, Tom passed by a woman by the name of Mabel. Her appearance was disturbing. She was blind, partly deaf, and half of her face had been eaten by cancer. She was so disturbing to look at that the head nurse would often send new nurses to feed Mabel as a test, figuring if they could endure working with Mabel, they could endure any challenge the facility had to offer.

Tom offered Mabel a flower one day, along with a word of encouragement. Mabel thanked him and asked if she could give the flower to someone else since she was blind. Over the next few years, Tom visited Mabel every week. Often, when the home was short-staffed, Mabel was placed with roommates who were not verbal and constantly soiled their beds. The smell caused many staff to quit, and Tom often wondered how Mabel could endure it without complaining. Not only did Mabel not complain, but she was giving and grateful, and she sang hymns with Tom whenever he came by.

Here is a woman who had clearly lived a life where she added value to others when she was healthy. Now, when she was weak, old, and ill, not a single person came to visit her, yet she never complained. When she was asked to change rooms, she would say, "I'd love it." One might question how she knew she loved it, knowing that she couldn't even see. She would respond lovingly, "Where you are has nothing to do with it. It has to do with me."

You may or may not be a person of faith, but I believe it still begs your attention to hear that faith was the center of Mabel's life. How could this be when for twenty-four hours per day, all month long, and twelve months per year, Mabel sat in darkness, listened to the groans of invalids, endured the smells of bodily fluids, and many times, due to shortness of staff, sat alone in her own soiled clothes for hours until someone could get to her?

Tom, who understood exactly what Mabel was enduring, once asked her what she thought about all day. She responded, "That's easy. I think about Jesus." Then she broke out in a hymn:

> Jesus is all the world to me,
> My life, my joy, my all;
> He is my strength from day to day,
> Without Him I would fall.
> When I am sad, to Him I go,
> No other one can cheer me so;
> When I am sad, He makes me glad,
> He's my Friend.

How we live life cannot only be reactionary. We are not only reactionary beings who are the results of the joys and traumas that we experience. Our lives are not determined by our positions; they are ultimately determined by the dispositions we choose. I am not denying how hard the trials and challenges of life are. Far from it. I am a firsthand witness that our experiences mark us in ways that can be life defining. Our experiences of elation and pain awaken us to the point of decision, and it is in that moment, when we come to a point of decision, that we can choose either to complain or to rejoice.

We Choose

The reality is that we have many more choices than we care to admit—and this exposes that most of us choose what we are used to. This choice gives us the least emotional pain. In the Western world, most people are neither rich nor poor; they are somewhere in the middle. Being in the middle, the American dream is socially preferable to being rich or poor. We criticize the rich and the poor. The choice to live in the economic middle, the middle of the pack, whether conscious or unconscious, is a choice. We are fearful of both the worries of the poor and the many concerns of the rich.

Those of us in the middle of the pack stand back and watch people who dedicate their lives to something greater than themselves, such as building an innovative business or challenging a world record. We observe with raised eyebrows those few who declare their intention to pursue a grand goal and make commitments toward it. We notice when these people face dire circumstances and either fail or succeed in their endeavors. We write about them as heroes for their wisdom if they achieve their goal or losers for their foolishness if they don't.

However, Theodore Roosevelt called them all great for choosing to pursue their dreams:

It is not the critic who counts; not the man who points out how the strong man stumbles, or where the doer of deeds could have done them better. The credit belongs to the man who is actually in the arena, whose face is marred by dust and sweat and blood; who strives valiantly; who errs, who comes short again and again because there is no effort without error and shortcoming; but who does actually strive to do the deeds; who knows great enthusiasms, the great devotions; who spends himself in a worthy cause; who at the best knows in the end the triumph of high achievement, and who at the worst, if he fails, at least fails while daring greatly, so that his place shall never be with those cold and timid souls who neither know victory nor defeat.[9]

An example of a great failure who eventually did well is Colonel Harland Sanders. The man who started the Kentucky Fried Chicken (KFC) franchise had a rough childhood, worked odd jobs in his early adult life, and bought and sold lackluster businesses until he tried to sell his "secret" fried chicken recipe to restaurants. At the age of sixty-five, with only a $105 Social Security check for means, he approached 1,009 restaurants before one said yes to his franchise idea.[10]

When we bet on ourselves and fail, we can rejoice because we tried. When we bet on ourselves and succeed, we can rejoice even more because we have become more than we have been. We may become larger-than-life or gain celebrity status. We honor celebrities and often make movies about them.

However, there is a dark side to seeing someone as a celebrity. In *Grit*, Angela Duckworth suggests that we enjoy making celebrities and then claiming that these people's results are due to natural talent or uncommon determination. We make heroes out of these people because it seems better than trying to hold ourselves to the same standard.[11]

Avoiding pursuing our dreams is a form of pain avoidance. Reaching for a goal is uncomfortable and may even involve pain. Then there are the everyday hurdles to jump at the same time. Pursuing our dreams can seem overwhelming.

The truth is that no matter how safe a height we aim for or how protected we believe we may be, tragedy hits us all. We will all lose someone we love or a job we cherish. A home will go up in flames or a hurricane will wipe out a life's earnings. These crucial moments become defining markers in our lives. These moments forge greatness or dissolve potential. When faced with painful, crucial moments, most people will choose to be one of four characters. Who you choose to be will shape your future:

The Escape Artist

This person will do anything they can to escape pain—no matter how they look or who it impacts. There is no integrity to hold firm the commitment of someone who is determined to get out of a painful situation.

The Complainer

Unfortunately, most people fall into this category when they feel powerless. Garnering pity is a form of borrowing power from others. Others choose to become victims of their pain by listening to them.

The Destroyer

Some people, when experiencing pain, find they have to create it somewhere else in order to feel like there is justice. It really doesn't matter if the target of their malevolence is responsible for their pain. Destroyers just have to express their pain somewhere.

The Rejoicer

This person experiences trials and chooses to look for the lessons learned, wins to celebrate, and good in life to appreciate. They are able to guard their hearts in a way that ensures a level of empowerment that is needed to be in control of their lives and to reach their goals.

The rejoicer is the person we can become if we so dare. The value to us in being a rejoicer is that we are in control of our lives and can maintain hope.

Choose Celebration

One of the most resilient groups of people on earth is the Jews. They are an ethnic group almost three thousand years old that extends to every part of the globe. Many leaders, including Pharaoh in Egypt, Xerxes in Persia, Nero in Rome, and Hitler in Germany have persecuted the Jews throughout history, yet most Jewish holidays are steeped in celebration.

Hanukkah is one of the most widely observed Jewish holidays. The minor festival commemorates the rededication of the Jerusalem temple in AD 165 and is a joyous eight-day celebration that falls during the darkest, coldest season of the year. Here is a people that, were it not for their insistence on celebrations, would probably have assimilated into most of the countries they inhabit. Yet, despite being persecuted, they have chosen celebrative practices that mark them as separate from all the other people in the world. They realize that when they stop their celebrating, there is no distinction.

One of the most heart-wrenching stories ever told was a story of the Jewish people. The 1959 film *The Diary of Anne Frank* recounts the true story of a family of Jews under persecution in Nazi Germany during World War II. The family hid from the Nazis in a secret annex for 761 days. After being found and arrested, they were soon killed.

But while in hiding, the Frank family still took time to rejoice during the eight days of Hanukkah. This commitment to continue to celebrate throughout dark days was a testament to their faith. In the film, Mrs. Frank says, "We thank thee, oh Lord our God, that in Thy infinite mercy Thou hast again seen fit to spare us. Come on, Anne, the song! Let's have the song."[12]

Choosing hope over fear and celebration over despair in times of trial is a choice. My hope is that you will make this choice to rejoice in your trials. Your celebration can give you happiness and make you distinct from a complainer.

It is counterintuitive to choose to rejoice when our world feels like it's upending. Panic is common when we are in a situation in which we feel we have no control, but we cannot afford to retreat in these moments. Our character is built in these moments. These moments empower us to direct our lives—not just live in them. We must choose in difficult moments to rejoice, to demonstrate that we are not victims of our circumstance, but writers of our destiny.

There's a biblical proverb that says, "If you falter in a time of trouble, how small is your strength."[13] This suggests that anyone can stand when not challenged, so we should not allow that to be a measure of the quality of our character. But to sing in times of trial, to celebrate when we feel low, to rejoice when all hell is breaking loose against us, this is the true measure of our character. The more we choose to rejoice in every circumstance, the more powerful we become.

Daily celebration is critical to reshaping your perspective on life. And reshaping your perspective is what you need to help you bounce back from any challenge.

PART III

EMBRACING THE DISCIPLINES IT TAKES TO WIN

THE BATTLE OF THE HANDS

REVITALIZING YOUR WORK

CHAPTER 9

REENGAGE

\rē-in-ˈgāj\

to participate in again[1]

The passage of time is all it takes to erode that initial impulse. Time is theft, isn't that what we say? … Time steals your nerve. If time and fear aren't enough to dissuade people … there's always authority, softly shaking its head and saying, "We understand, but you're a better man for letting it go. For rising above it. For not sinking to their level" …
You know I'm right. You know there's a lot of work to do. It may seem impossible, but I'm sure if we all do our part, we'll figure something out. But you don't have much time. You've only got about ten minutes, in fact. Then it starts all over again. So do something with the time you've got.
—**Nathan Nolan, "Memento Mori"**[2]

Failure is not falling down, but refusing to get up.
—**Chinese proverb**[3]

I thought I was going to die. No, not figuratively, but literally. I was only ten years old, and I was focused on trying to breathe. *What is happening to me? Is this what asthma feels like? Am I about to die?*

One moment, I was playing basketball, and the next moment, I took an elbow right above my gut and into my solar plexus. I couldn't breathe and fell to the ground. Gym teachers see this happen to students often, and it can cause them to laugh, but for me, who had spent the past decade on the planet with full access to my lungs, this experience was akin to the Grim Reaper coming early. For the first time in my life, I had the wind knocked out of me.

During those moments, where seconds felt like minutes and minutes felt like hours, students and adults created a circle around me. Some had looks of panic, while others looked thrilled; this was one of the most exciting things to happen in gym class. They yelled, "Just breathe!" With both my mouth and nose wide-open, I was trying.

How Long Will You Stay Down?

Most extremely difficult and challenging circumstances in life have the power to knock the proverbial wind right out of us. What you will notice during these times is how similar all the voices that surround us sound—much like they did on that day when I was in distress with my childhood muscle spasm.

Some people find your pain entertaining. This is clear when you consider the rise of hundreds of reality shows, such as *The Bachelor* and *Married at First Sight*, which all but guarantee they will profit from someone's pain. No doubt, there are a few observers who are concerned and desire to help—but not enough to do anything significant. There also are people who are truly concerned yet offer incredibly unhelpful advice.

Regardless of what people say, what matters most in these trying circumstances is not the advice you hear or the knowledge you possess; it is how long it takes for you to recover and reengage in the fight. At ten, I sat out the rest of the class period, thinking that my experience carried with it some kind of warning of what may happen in the future.

This was an emotional calculation and not a logical one. The elephant in me was hurt, and it chose the path of disengagement. Without an override command to keep going despite the feeling, the elephant will refuse to continue in the fight. The principle of reengagement teaches that failure is inevitable—but not final. The choice to keep fighting is the only option if you are to achieve your dreams.

As a kid, I played basketball hundreds of times, and getting the wind knocked out of me happened only one time. A logical analysis of these events would suggest I had at least another decade and hundreds more games before this would happen again. That's assuming I took no protective measures moving forward.

Too often, people decide after being fired, failing in business, or experiencing a painful divorce that they will never try again. They sit out of the game, just like me at ten, psychologically recovering from a minor injury, lacking the will to get back in and give 100 percent.

Some will get back in the game, but they will no longer play all-out in order to win. Instead of playing to win, they start playing not to lose. They play with a psychological disability that seeks to protect them from feeling the pain they previously experienced. It's like playing football and protecting an arm so as not to injure it. This practice of playing not to get hurt reduces our efforts and weakens our resolve to win. To win, we must be committed to looking ahead and releasing the pain from before. Releasing the pain could mean moving past it, forgetting it, ignoring it, or working through it.

> Do not judge me by my success, judge me by how
> many times I fell down and got back up again.
> **—Nelson Mandela**[4]

Too Stupid to Fail

It is said that a great golfer has a long memory for the good shots and a short memory for the bad ones, and an amateur has the exact opposite problem. As an amateur golfer, I can tell you this is true. As I coach leaders, I consistently hear flawed belief systems that stagnate progress and invite defeat. I once coached a business leader who suggested to me that the current downturn in his business must be a sign that he was growing too fast and needed to slow down. Some business leaders used spiritual reasons, saying that God was trying to tell them something. Others described fate as having a hand in their situations.

What's amazing to me is that this reaction of reading meaning into events tends to happen only when things are going wrong. I never hear these people using the good things that happen as a sign to take their profits and go to Las Vegas to try their fortunes at the blackjack table. In most cases, when things are going well or not, it's simply the nature and rhythm of business. In this chapter, I want to challenge you to stop trying to make meaning out of everything.

It takes courage for spiritual leaders to speak out against over-spiritualizing everything. One spiritual leader I respect is Andy Stanley. In his talk on momentum, he confronts leaders to take responsibility for the consequences of their actions and not to blame God. Stanley concedes that God is blessing a church when things are going well. But if God were just randomly choosing churches to bless, then wouldn't he just bless all of them? There are churches that pray more, worship more, and have good moral leadership, but they spend decades with no growth and even declining membership. Other churches with questionable theology thrive.

Stanley challenges leaders to consider exactly what God is blessing. He contends that God does not bless at random or bless only the most spiritual. He acknowledges specific leadership principles that, if followed, would result in any church being blessed.[5]

This reinforces one of my favorite quotes by Jim Collins:

"Disciplined people who engage in disciplined thought and who take disciplined action are the cornerstone of a culture that creates greatness."[6]

We have to trade our superstitious beliefs about events, and we must trust the process Jim Collins taught. If we reengage as disciplined people—with disciplined thought and disciplined action—we will achieve almost any result. This means experiencing the grief of the moment—but refusing to chart the rest of the journey based on it.

Our elephant is too smart, and its intuition is too attentive to ignore the pain of failure and rejection of yesterday. Therefore, we need to develop a deep conviction that chooses ignorance over awareness. We need to numb our responsiveness to the pain and act as if it were impossible to fail. We literally need to play stupid when it comes to the fear of rejection and failure, and then we must continue with the same level of grit and enthusiasm as when we first started.

Motivational speaker Les Brown tells the story of wanting to be a radio disc jockey at the beginning of his career. At the same time, he was coached by a mentor never to accept other people's opinions of him as self-defining. So, he showed up four days in a row at a radio station asking for a job where he was told three times that there were no available positions. When he came back each day to ask, the radio station manager, Mr. Butterball, would ask why he continued to come back. Les would respond that he didn't know if anyone was fired, got sick, or died.

Finally, on day four of Les showing up and asking for a job as if for the first time, Mr. Butterball gave in and offered him a job. Les will tell you it doesn't matter how many times you are refused; it's how many times you bounce back. "Don't be afraid if you land on your back," he says. "If you can look up, you can get up."[7]

From Regret to Resilience

Regret is one of the strongest feelings people have as they get older. Some people feel guilty for things they have left undone. Others feel regret for not doing what they feel they should have done given their skills, talents, and abilities. For still others, these feelings strike as midlife crises.

There is a now disorder called *quarter-life crisis*, in which people in their midtwenties start to feel as if they are lost due to a lack of results or not achieving what they think they should. In addition to regret, the awareness of our mortality, our limited reach, and the temporary impact of everything we do can weigh on us and create a lot of negative feelings, which can keep us down.

We must learn the art of rising up after being knocked down—in other words, the art of reengaging. Reengagement is the process that we go through to overcome our fears, doubts, and inaction. With reengagement, we can push forward, no matter what's ahead.

Bonnie St. John said, "Resilience is the power or ability to return to the original form … after being bent, compressed, or stretched … But we believe that normal is not good enough; we focus instead on ways to bounce back better than normal."[9]

Thankful for Scars

One person who reengaged after a setback was Eric Liddell, the 1924 Olympic gold medal winner in the 400-meter race. Liddell trained for the Olympics while he was at the University of Edinburgh in Scotland, but his path to the university from Eltham College, where he studied in his teenage years, was not straight. His time at Eltham College left him short of a full credit in the French language, so he did not enter university the fall after he graduated. He needed to revitalize his study skills to progress to the next level.

Liddell spent the summer after graduating from Eltham College studying with a French tutor. He spent that fall at Heriot-Watt College studying more French, along with various other subjects. Liddell obtained a Scottish Universities Entrance Board Certificate in February 1921. It was then that his extra studying with the French tutor and at Heriot-Watt paid off. He officially entered the University of Edinburgh on February 23, 1921, and his road to the Olympics began.[10]

Now, most would look at Liddell's setback and assume that he achieved all that he did despite his challenges. But when you consider the volumes of literature we have on accomplished people, it's more likely that he achieved greatness because of the setback. We are learning that for most of us, it is the adversity itself that creates the opportunity and shapes us for greatness. It may seem silly to rejoice in all circumstances, but it turns out to be the recipe for success.

Rejoicing in all circumstances puts you in the best mindset to solve problems and to work with people to solve problems. Zig Ziglar said, "Others can stop you temporarily. You are the only one who can do it permanently."[11] Staying in a good mood during challenging times gives you the energy to keep going.

In a teaching moment, John Maxwell once quoted the *Los Angeles Times*, "If you can smile whenever anything goes wrong, you are either a nitwit or a repairman." He added, "Or a leader in the making—one who realizes that the only problem you have is the one you allow to be a problem because of your wrong reaction to it."[12] A leader's job is to help people through the problems. Smiling and showing your good nature during a problem calms your people and reassures them that you are safe to follow.

When we're deciding whether to reengage or not, the biggest obstacle is rarely a physical hurdle; it's usually an emotional and/or mental one. For example, a door-to-door salesperson has to go out and suffer rejection, hour after hour and day after day, but they're never physically threatened. Those who do well consistently are paid well, but they suffer a lot of rejection along the way. In spite of that, they do what unsuccessful people are unwilling to do; they keep going after being told no, and they constantly reengage.

I was a salesman for part of my career. I started out at Nordstrom in Minneapolis, and in my department store sales role, I soon realized that, as humans, we are often too easily satisfied. I think that's one of the challenges with human nature; satisfaction puts us in a place of comfort, and our comfort lulls us into complacency. Then we're not engaging in our daily activities to our full potential. This is what happened to my colleagues at Nordstrom. They would work hard when they knew a sale was coming up, but they didn't apply that same mentality to their everyday work.

Contrary to them, at the beginning of the first full year I worked at Nordstrom, I set a goal to become a "Pacesetter," which was something that hadn't been achieved in the history of the Minneapolis store. A Pacesetter was someone who made enough sales to be in the top 3 percent of the salespeople within the national company.

Coworkers gave all types of excuses as to why there couldn't be a Pacesetter in my store. The reasoning went like this. We were in a medium-sized store, which had a medium amount of foot traffic, but it required a full staff. Smaller stores with fewer salespeople but higher foot traffic had Pacesetters on their staffs. Larger stores had more salespeople, but they were also flooded with foot traffic, so they had Pacesetters on their staff. So, the small stores, like the one in Salt Lake City, Utah, would always over perform because they kept just enough people on deck, but they also had enough traffic to produce Pacesetters. In a middle market like Minneapolis, we had a medium amount of foot traffic, being in a medium-sized city, but we had a full staff. And so, my colleagues believed that the Pacesetter goal could not be accomplished in Minnesota.

But what I did on the first of January that year was determine how much I needed to sell every day in the coming year to become a Pacesetter. I wrote down on each day in my planner what I needed to sell, and I did this for the entire year. When I would over perform, I wouldn't change the planner to lower my goals. But when I would underperform, I would go through my entire year and determine how many days I needed to raise my goal in order to stay on track.

By the end of October, I did something that no one else in my store had ever done: I hit that top 3 percent of the salespeople in the company. And I still had two full months to break and set many new records that stayed for a very long time. My idea worked. When everybody else would disengage, when things would slow down, I continued working at an optimal level. My commitment to reengage after every sale gave me the power to perform at a high level—no matter what was going on around me.

Tim Grover's *Relentless: From Good to Great to Unstoppable* used his experiences from working as a physical trainer for Michael Jordan, Kobe Bryant, Dwayne Wade, and many other high-level athletes. He noticed that there was definitely something different about these top performers.[13]

Michael Jordan, Grover said, worked harder than any man he'd ever known. Jordan practiced more diligently than the athletes around him; he practiced for hours on end before team practice, and then he practiced with his team. Then he would expect all of his teammates to stay late in order to focus on the goal of staying fully engaged at all times. Grover said that Michael Jordan was "in the zone" more than any other player he's ever worked with. Jordan would play every game in the zone. He would get to that place where he would literally control and dominate a game. That doesn't happen if you are too easily satisfied.

And that's why, unlike most other athletes, Michael Jordan won six championships in six years. He was willing to give an extraordinary level of commitment to his craft. Now, of course, he took a couple years off for baseball. But in his last six full seasons playing with the Chicago Bulls, he won championships every year. Very few athletes win championships back-to-back, and a select elite accomplish a three-peat. But here's an athlete who won six seasons in a row—a three-peat twice. That's a rigorous amount of reengagement.[14]

Everyone Can Reengage

Everybody has the ability to reengage, but there are four main reasons why we don't. First, we may need to overcome the emotional degradation that happens when we feel defeated. Second, we may struggle to reengage because we don't want to continue to be knocked down. Third, as I mentioned before, some people get comfortable working at a low level. Fourth, some people may not have good mental models that allow them to push through and push forward.

Environment also plays a role in reengagement. People might not be in an environment in which the expectation is for full-blown engagement and staying "in the zone" no matter what. One of the challenges we face is figuring out how to build habits that engage us at this level of intensity. We need to build habits that keep us engaged—even when our minds need time for rest and recovery.

Although we can appreciate celebrities like Eric Liddell and Michael Jordan, one thing we do know is that our work is different from theirs. They practice 80–90 percent of the time, but they only play for sixty minutes a game. The difference for us is that we are engaged in our work 90 percent of the time with very little time, if any, set aside for practice.

Give Yourself the Power to Reengage

So, how do we get done what we need to do? How do we keep the different parts of ourselves sharp when we're feeling fatigue? In *Micro-Resilience*, Bonnie St. John and Allen Haines explain five strategies that empower people to stay engaged for long periods of time. They explain in detail ways that people can refocus their brains, reset their primitive alarms, reframe their attitudes, refresh their bodies, and renew their spirits.[15]

When I was a sales trainer for Qwest Corporation, I had the privilege of challenging the mental models of the salespeople in the three lowest-performing stores. Qwest had developed a commission system that supported the salespeople's ability to essentially be lazy for two or three months until their goals lowered so significantly that they could easily sell three to four times their sales goals and, in doing so, receive large commissions. But if they performed well several months in a row, then their sales goals would become so high that they wouldn't make commission anymore. The salespeople at these three stores had figured out that they would make more money being lazy than by working hard.

My job as a sales trainer was to get them all performing at the highest level they possibly could. So, I challenged all three sales teams to consider this: that no company compensating them for underperformance will be in business long. And if they continued to go down this path, their skills would eventually diminish. I told them it was in their best interests to show up every day to work at the top of their skill levels because those skills would be necessary no matter where they went in their careers. I challenged them to live according to their potential.

Over the next year, these salespeople went from underperforming to over performing. Each one of their stores, at different times, became the number one store in the nation for sales. My challenge to their salespeople was to reengage every day and to work not just for what their current jobs demanded of them but for what their futures would demand of them.

Along those same lines is our mission statement here at Experience Leadership: "We are committed to exploring the limits of your potential by releasing the unique gifts within you and expressing them through business success." If you want to be successful, you need to have this almost trampoline-like experience; whenever you get pushed down or deal with any type of idea that has to do with reality, you must be willing and able to bounce back.

Our bodies, minds, and spirits go through a dynamic shift when we reengage. When we stay engaged, an *invigoration* takes place. More adrenaline and norepinephrine flow into our bloodstreams at these times, which allows us to get excited. Psychologist Mihaly Csikszentmihalyi's *Flow* lays out a theory that underperformance and low performance send us toward depression.[16]

In contrast, as we put ourselves into situations that are more challenging and more exciting for us, we begin to engage at a much higher level, which gives us the adrenaline and the norepinephrine we need to accomplish great things. And so, in those moments in which we are deciding whether to reengage or not, it's in our best interests to reengage and act.

As I've explained in several chapters, our minds operate off of pictures. Picture the reengagement principle as a trampoline, as I suggested above. A trampoline gives us the ability to use the force that pushes us down to bounce back stronger and better.

For those who are still wondering what I learned after having the air knocked out of me in fifth grade, well, I learned to never stay down again.

CHAPTER 10

REFINE

/rəˈfīn/

Improve (something) by making small changes[1]

Without continual growth and progress, such words as
improvement, achievement, and success have no meaning.
—Benjamin Franklin[2]

You cannot travel within and stand still without.
—James Allen[3]

One of the most difficult experiences of my young adult life was the day I ran for freshman class president in college. I was egged on to participate in the political race by the previous year's freshman class president. He knew me from high school, and he mentioned that the charisma and energy he saw in me would make me "a shoo-in." He convinced me it would be easy.

My friend from high school actually even helped me campaign. He taught me how to politic around as he had done the previous year. I went around meeting people, trying to be likeable, and letting people know what was at stake in the election.

As we went through dormitory hallways shaking students' hands (there were no babies to kiss), we made it known that I was running for class president and would make a great one. We even began introducing me as the next freshman class president. It was all very exciting. I began to believe my own press. I thought I would be the natural favorite. I had no desire to do any negative campaigning, but I can't say my opponents all followed suit.

At the conclusion of the campaign, the freshmen needed to pick their president—but not before hearing from the candidates themselves. There were three candidates who made the final cut to speak and be voted on.

The first candidate was a young lady, and I could see from the looks on the faces of the crowd during her speech that they were not interested in her. She seemed nice enough, but she gave off a vibe that said, "I should be president because I prevented senior ditch day by reporting it to the principal." Her speaking ability was okay, but I absolutely knew she didn't win the students over.

I was the second candidate to speak. *This is going to be a walk in the park,* I thought. You see, I had been a public speaker for more than a decade. Between church talks, drama, and my wins on eighth-grade debate team, I knew the other candidates didn't stand a chance. I was confident I would outperform the others and win the students' votes.

In my speech, I spoke of the university's charge to shape the values of us as future world leaders. I emphasized that I believed in my fellow students, and as their class president, I would look for ways to add value to them. I did my best to combine the inspiration of Les Brown and Zig Ziglar with the intellectualization of Stephen Covey and John Maxwell and roll them into one stump speech. (I will neither confirm nor deny that there may have been speaker's plagiarism involved.) I thought I did great, and the crowd clapped widely for me.

Third and finally, a gentleman from Kentucky rose to speak.

He had a golden voice with a southern drawl. He captivated people with his stories and jokes. His speech was charming, his timing was impeccable, and his sense of humor was crowd-pleasing. He got them laughing. Then, he brought out of them compassion and tears with an incredible story. He drew the students all into a religious fervor like a televangelist. He made me think I wanted to vote for him.

And, boy, was that disappointing. I knew then that when the final votes were tallied, he would be victorious. And my disappointment was confirmed later that evening when he won in a landslide.

At first, I was pretty upset. It was clear to me that someone had brought in a ringer—this man from Kentucky. How old was he? He definitely couldn't be a freshman. This guy hadn't spoken to the voters previously. He hadn't campaigned at all. I didn't even realize he was on the ballot until I came to the auditorium in the evening.

And then I had to face all the people I had told I would be the next president. Talk about humble pie. I guess the biggest disappointment for me wasn't that the man from Kentucky was a more effective communicator than me. The biggest disappointment for me was that I realized how much work went into actually giving a rousing talk. I realized that day that I had never taken advantage of the head start I received in life.

In *The E-Myth Revisited,* Michael Gerber said, "Some people think they have twenty years' experience when what they actually have is one year of experience repeated twenty times."[4] Just to think that years earlier, I could have been working on improving my speaking skill rather than assuming from a fixed mindset that I was naturally talented—and that was enough.

You see, I started speaking in front of people when I was eight years old. Back then, people celebrated me for being such a young person with the conviction and courage to get up there and speak publicly. That led to drama and speech classes, the debate team, and many other clubs and events that I participated in over the next few years. I would get up there and give it my best go, and people were consistently impressed.

Because of all the praise I received early on, I made the blunder of believing somehow that my speaking skills were at their optimum when, in fact, I was still operating with my eight-year-old skill set. I hadn't done anything in ten years to improve or increase my impact. Looking back, to tell the truth, I was pretty average as a communicator. My only real advantage was that I had the courage and confidence to stand in front of people.

The freshman class president campaign made me realize how good I could have been had I sought to improve my speaking ability year after year. Instead, I coasted along, believing what everyone else said about me. I thought I was a good communicator simply because people were impressed with my courage to speak in front of an audience.

Looking at Your Future

How does my freshman class president story relate to you? Maybe you've recently found out you're not as talented as you thought you were, as I did as a college freshman. Maybe you've struggled all along with feeling inadequate or not being good enough to reach your goals. Let's take a look at how you can change your situation.

The biggest room in the world is the room for improvement.
—Helmut Schmidt[5]

A refinery is a production facility where a company uses chemicals and special equipment to convert raw materials into something with product value. It makes sense that companies would refine oils, gases, sugars, salts, metals, and stones because we realize all these things in their raw state are not as useful or beautiful as when they are refined. Could you imagine people fighting over who has the best-looking raw gold nugget? No one but miners would truly be interested in looking at such a thing. We only admire the look of gold when it is refined: purified, shiny, and smooth.

I often hear people who are not invested in personal development arguing over who has the most raw talent. The truth is that it doesn't matter. I, personally, don't want to hear the singer, watch the athlete, or look at the art of the person who was the best before being trained. Show me the power that comes from the sweat, blood, and tears of sleepless effort.

A few years ago, I read Jeff Olson's *The Slight Edge.* Olson suggests that most people could easily improve their finances, health, and relationships if they would only take small, proactive steps every day to move in the direction of progress.[7]

Physical health provides an easy example. Some people go to the gym consumed with the shape and functionality of their bodies. They become obsessed with their bodies. But the reality is that most gym memberships go unused.[8] The person with the unused gym membership has the intention of improving their health, but their direction is in the opposite way. They are not taking proactive steps to improve their health, and this harms them.

Then there's dieting, which in the United States in 2019 was a $72 billion industry as people lost weight, gained it back, and lost it again.[9] It makes you want to ask, "If so many people are concerned about their bodies, why don't they do something about it permanently?"

I realize that heredity and genetics have something to do with how our bodies are shaped, but the primary causes for the shapes and strengths of our bodies are what we put in our mouths and the activities we do, both of which we have control over.

Take, for example, one of my mentors. When someone asked him how he lost more than 130 pounds in a year, he said that it had been very, very simple. He explained that for ten years, he had constantly drunk beer and eaten whatever he saw that appealed to him. Then, one day, he simply stopped. As funny as this sounds, it's amazing how much truth it contains.

In the pursuit of refinement, we must first determine where we would like to be. We will never reach perfection, but the lack of perfection should not be an excuse to neglect its pursuit. Vince Lombardi said, "Perfection is not attainable. But if we chase perfection, we can catch excellence."[10]

I believe excellence is developed in three steps:

- Preparation: Set clear goals and a method for measuring progress
- Organization: Define actions that will lead to achievement
- Activation: Become obsessed with refining the process

Preparation

One of the elements you won't find in achievement-oriented people is mediocrity. If mediocrity is your goal, I am surprised you made it this far in the book. For goal attainment, there can be no room for average effort. We must develop a burning desire, as Napoleon Hill said, to go after the goals we are chasing.[11] Anyone can set goals, but it takes a person with a burning desire to achieve them. Achievement-oriented people must be clear on their values, clear on their goals, and have already settled with themselves the price they are willing to pay to live their values and attain their goals.

Let's look beyond the individual to some of the most successful companies in the world. They are often driven to proclaim a very distinct set of values. If we are committed to building something of lasting value, we have to get extremely clear on the impact we want to make.

In *The Infinite Game*, Simon Sinek opens with the contrast between the games that were being played by Microsoft and Apple during the same year. His observation was that when he spoke at Microsoft, they were focused on a fixed timetable to outperform their fiercest competition, Apple. Within a few months, Sinek went to speak at Apple. They were fixated on something very different. Leaders at Apple were consumed with how they were helping teachers teach and students learn.[12] Sinek observed:

> The true value of an organization is measured by
> the desire others have to contribute to that organi-
> zation's ability to keep succeeding, not just during
> the time they are there, but well beyond their own
> tenure.[13]

At the end of the day, long-term success hinges on leaders committing to refinement: the continual discovery and execution of their
values and the increasing development of their skills. Improvement
in these areas comes not from thinking about how to make more
money but from thinking about how to better serve more people.

> Measurement is the first step that leads to control and
> eventually to improvement. If you can't measure something,
> you can't understand it. If you can't understand it, you can't
> control it. If you can't control it, you can't improve it.
> **—H. James Harrington[14]**

Pick a measurement method that agrees with what you are trying
to improve. One method that has worked well down through the ages
is the scientific method shown below:

> Observe → Make Hypothesis → Test Hypothesis and
> Collect Data → Analyze Results → Accept or Reject
> Hypothesis → Repeat

The scientific method is applicable to a variety of situations. You
most likely will be able to apply it to what you want to improve.

Organization

Refining our lifestyle involves a full commitment to self-betterment.
This commitment has the most long-term impact when we make

small strokes toward constant improvement. Small improvements have the most impact when they become daily habits. Sustainable daily habits will take us where we ultimately want to go.

This is why I am fully convinced that the most powerful move we can make for our health is to take small, repeatable steps toward better health. Just a little bit every day. This bettering of ourselves can be applied to other areas of our lives, such as work, with similar positive results. A whole host of greats in the field of success agree with me.

In *The Slight Edge*, Jeff Olson points out that a lot of people are going after quantum leap changes in life. But these quantum leaps, such as winning the lottery or getting a surprise promotion, don't materialize that often. The guaranteed way to truly change your life is to change your daily habits.[15]

John Maxwell says something similar in *Today Matters*. He goes over twelve disciplines required to live a successful, effective life. He defines success as something that is hidden in your daily agenda.[16]

Further, in Maxwell's *The 15 Invaluable Laws of Growth*, he shares the law of the mirror: you must see value in yourself to add value to yourself.[17] If you don't realize that you have genuine value and that you are worth investing in, then you will never put in the time and effort needed to grow to your potential. Many people have lost confidence in their ability to achieve because of the assumptions about achievement they picked up along the way.

In *Mindset*, Carol Dweck, a Stanford professor, suggests that many people have set themselves up for failure when it comes to self-improvement because they have embraced a fixed mindset. A person with a fixed mindset believes that the game is ultimately set and that the results can't really be improved. These people have abandoned the opportunity for growth in exchange for the mindset that massive improvements can't be made.[18]

The fact is, says Dweck, you will be willing to go out and make yourself better when you possess the belief that you actually can become better. She really attacks the idea that a person cannot improve.[19]

Then there's the idea that natural talent is overrated, which Geoff Colvin explores in his aptly titled *Talent Is Overrated*. In his research for the book, Colvin and his team traveled the United States looking for the innate talent of superstars, but they couldn't find any. They did meet people who were good and naturally good, but when they looked at the mastery of something, the only people who truly mastered things had spent well over ten thousand hours practicing.[20]

Daniel Coyle's *The Talent Code* also gets to the heart of mastery. Coyle refers to a person being able to master something through the process of *deliberate practice*. The book reveals that talent isn't the determining factor when it comes to true mastery. What distinguishes one talented person from another is deliberate practice, which translates into having an intentional process to make yourself better.[21]

The Talent Code further explores the science behind why practice matters. Coyle explains that when we practice a skill, the myelin sheath grows thicker around the relevant nerve cells. For the athlete, the myelin sheath grows thicker around the nerve cells that are important in directing muscles. For Albert Einstein, the myelin sheath was thick around the nerve cells in the prefrontal cortex of his brain.[22]

Dweck reinforces the science behind mastery at any age by describing the brain's ability to continually change, which is referred to as *neuroplasticity*. Contrary to what the American media portrays, some people in their later years have more mental activity than they had in their younger years. Dweck writes that it was discovered that when these people were young, they believed they would keep learning and growing as they aged—so they kept learning and growing as they aged. This is true in other pockets of the world too. When people from these places are in their nineties, their brains are just as active as they were in their forties.[23]

To explain this idea, Dweck shows a recursive arrow for the person with a growth mindset. When this person experiences a challenge or failure, they press through it and achieve higher. Their higher achievement causes them to perform better, and that validates their process: that someone who works hard presses through challenges. And the process reinforces their belief that they can improve.[24]

Let's step back and look at the person with a fixed mindset. When they experience challenge and failure, they give less effort because they assume that if they're not good at it now, they won't get better, so there's no reason to try to push through. They stop working as hard. They don't want to go all in because it's out of their comfort zone, which is what they believe their skill level is. They might say, "I'm not good at it." With a fixed mindset, they perform less, and their lower performance has a recursive effect, which validates their fixed mindset.

But, as we've seen, many experts say talent isn't a fixed thing. If it isn't determined by what you already bring to the table, there must be a shift in our beliefs that we can become better. Dweck challenges people to embrace a growth mindset, to believe that challenge and failure aren't bad, and to believe we can create better lives for ourselves. But we need to focus our energy and make our practice deliberate. That's the process of refinement from a growth mindset.[25]

The growth mindset really solidifies that if you believe you can get better, you will. If you have full confidence that failure is not final—and that it is just part of the pat—you can feel energized to start employing growth habits. You say, "Okay, I can get better." You commit to refining yourself and making small, daily improvements. You say, "I just want to be a little bit better. I want to be the best version of myself."

What about me and my ability to make speeches? As an adult, I have taken steps to improve my public speaking ability. I took the Dale Carnegie and John Maxwell speaking courses. I often spend weeks preparing for my speaking engagements instead of just giving it my best go. And because of these actions, I've improved enough to know that I'm a good speaker.

It's okay if you don't reach your goals overnight, but you can organize your life to improve a little bit every day. To improve, throw yourself into challenges in order to get feedback, which will help you understand what your next steps should be.

Activation

At this point in the book, I hope I have highlighted how strongly a person's beliefs control their behaviors. We must embrace a mindset that lets our beliefs work for us. The fact is, you will be willing to go out of your way to make yourself better if you are completely committed to the belief that you can become better.

In *The Slight Edge*, Olson states that people are on one of two paths: they are either a hero or a victim of the slight edge. On the one hand, the hero of the slight edge story realizes that daily disciplines and systematic practice achieves for them a certain level of excellence with any endeavor or any goal they set for themselves. On the other hand, the person who is the habitual underachiever or the victim of the slight edge is that way because their daily disciplines, practices, or habits leave them in a place where they will be irreversibly unable to attain their goals.[26]

And the slight edge is tricky because, above all, you have to realize that there is only a subtle daily difference between the victim story and the hero story. One example would be looking at what a person on a journey to becoming a victim would eat compared to what that person on a journey to becoming a hero to himself would eat. The person as a hero says to himself, "I want to take care of my body, so I won't eat that cheeseburger today." The person as a victim says, "I don't care. I'm going to eat the cheeseburger." Neither gives two thoughts about it.

But what about the person who is just lacking willpower? Life requires, sometimes, that we make moment-by-moment decisions. At other times, we need to ask for help to achieve our goals, to make the decisions that are right for us. Sometimes we need to do both.

We deceive ourselves into thinking that the consequences of those decisions are so small that it doesn't seem to matter which choice we make that day. In reality, the person who eats the cheeseburger will not die tomorrow because of that cheeseburger. They probably could eat that cheeseburger every day for the next year, and they would be mostly unchanged.

Likewise, the hero who doesn't eat the cheeseburger does not miraculously and quickly emerge as a specimen of health. Like I said, starting out, there is only a subtle difference between the victim who eats the cheeseburger and the hero who doesn't.

Instead, there is a buildup of consequences. The person who reads a book today doesn't become a genius tomorrow. The person who neglects to read today doesn't suddenly have a vast vacuum of intellect.

The difficulty with the slight edge is that no matter what decision you make, for or against, it doesn't seem as if it makes a difference in the moment that you make the decision. And that's the deception. Jeff Olson refers to that as a simple error in judgment.[27] There is a simple error in judgment because it doesn't seem as if making the choice one way or the other makes a difference today.

However, over time, the gap widens between a person who is habitually making the wrong decisions and a person who is habitually making the right decisions. This gap widens after a certain amount of time and grows into a vast separation.

Between the beginning of a slight edge story and the day the vast separation is realized, there's an exponential curve of consequences. The negative consequences compound like interest on a loan. At first, compounding interest doesn't seem like much, but over time, it really adds up.[28] In the same way, three years from now, if you eat a cheeseburger daily, it may turn into an extra 140 pounds. However, not eating that cheeseburger daily and instead embracing good habits may turn into a very healthy lifestyle.

The commitment to success—to building ourselves up and fully becoming who we want to be—requires constant refinement, whether it be in health, the social realm, or business.

This chapter adds another voice to the chorus of success masters saying that reaching our goals starts with good daily habits. We can gain good, sustainable daily habits through preparing our minds, organizing our environments, and committing ourselves to those habits.

CONCLUSION

REMAIN

/rəˈmān/

Stand your ground, and having done everything, to stand. Stand!
—The apostle Paul

Commitment is doing the thing you said you were going
to do long after the mood you said it in has left you.
—Darren Hardy

There is a game I liked to play whenever I would take my children to Chuck E. Cheese. It's a game that represents a test of endurance. You grab the bars with two hands, and after you press the start button, it starts to give off a strong vibration to test how long you can hang on. Maybe one of the reasons I liked it so much was because, in the eyes of my kids who could barely hang on for more than a few seconds, I actually looked like a hero. Yes, for some reason, I was bigger than life for a moment.

As I reflect on these precious moments and the hundreds like it where they looked at me with admiring eyes, it was things like showing them how to ride a bike, teaching their Sunday school class, or speaking fluent Spanish to a stranger in a store. These moments bring me back to the heart of the questions and the only one that really matters. After all is said and done and my life is dead and gone, I want to know, what will remain? I decided that what strangers think of me has become a lot less important than the moments I create with my children, the people I impact and serve, and what they will become when I am no longer around to guide them.

What Truly Remains?

Some way or another, we are going to leave this earth. Death is the one human experience that none of us can escape. However, when you think of death, what is really going on? There are many things that leave—and some that remain. Your body remains; memories remain as long as those whom you've influenced are alive. Recordings of you, whether in video, audio, or written form, will last, but only as long those devices, books, or technologies last. People like Dr. Martin Luther King Jr. have died young (age thirty-nine) and have impacted generations, while others have lived more than a century and very few will ever know their names. In the Broadway musical *Hamilton*, Lin-Manuel Miranda gives an incredible depiction of a young man (Alexander Hamilton) who always lived, wrote, and worked like he was running out of time.

Time is a funny thing. In the eyes of history, things that are so significant in a day, a year, or even a decade will often be washed away in the sands of time. The victories of a World Series, a World Cup, or a world war are relatively significant, depending on the frame of reference. In any given generation, there are hundreds of millions who have become celebrities, including actors, musicians, authors, playwrights, YouTube stars, athletes, news anchors, business tycoons, war heroes, religious leaders, pageant winners, and dare I mention even politicians. Yet with all the noise that will be made within a year, how much of it will matter? If you think of the terms often used when it comes to the impact or effect of one's actions, they are often words like "weight," "gravity," and "matter." What determines if the events or the actions of an individual have any weight or actually matter?

If I am going to leave the mark that I want to leave in the world, it won't be because of my athletic prowess or my intellectual contributions. That's not my calling. My contribution will be that I loved enough to make a difference in the trajectory of people's lives, that I loved enough to overcome my own pride, and that I was willing to do things that other people wouldn't do to make a significant difference in the lives of others.

The Shock of Tragedy

Depending on your age and place in the world, you will remember exactly where you were when you heard of the deaths of the people listed below:

- John F. Kennedy
- Dr. Martin Luther King Jr.
- Elvis Presley
- John Elton
- Jimi Hendrix
- Marvin Gaye
- Michael Jackson
- Whitney Houston
- Heath Ledger
- Kobe Bryant
- Chadwick Boseman

TO be honest, I don't remember where I was when Zig Ziglar died. I can't tell you what I was doing when Ronald Reagan, Neil

Armstrong, or Jim Rohn died, which all occurred in my lifetime. The reason may not surprise you: I have little recollection of those events for these larger-than-life people because I believed they had lived out their usefulness.

In the end, it's not the years in your life that
count. It's the life in your years.
—Edward J. Stieglitz

In 2019, my grandmother transitioned from this life into eternity. I was the grandson who was selected to give her eulogy, and with full passion, I talked from the passage of scripture that reflected her life, 1 Corinthians 13:13: "And now these three remain: faith, hope and love. But the greatest of these is love." I was able to eulogize how she modeled these practices for us and how it made a difference in shaping her eight children, fifty-four grandchildren, and more than two hundred great-grandchildren. Because she *remained* steady in character and firm in her faith, we all knew exactly who she was— and we were given a road map to better form our lives.

I cried that I would miss my grandmother, but it was not a tear of heartbreak. It was a tear of rejoicing, knowing that she died empty, as Myles Munroe would say, leaving it all on the line. The impact of grief and loss is severely impacted by how much was lost and how much remains.

I was also scheduled to give words at the funeral of one of my cousins. Kenneth (Kenny) Frederick Fuller was one of my closest cousins growing up. Since he was eleven months younger than me, we were a natural pair on trips, camps, and in back seats of cars. Due to some family issues, they would sometimes move out of town. When they moved to Evanston, Illinois, I would go and visit him. In high school, I was able to sneak into his homecoming dance by using his school ID because we looked so much alike. During my college years, his family moved to Oklahoma, and I lost contact with him.

I will never forget where I was when I got the call. I was in the restroom in a crowded place, and I was trying to wash my hands as my cousin said, "Kenny is dead." I wasn't sure I heard him right, so I rushed out of the restroom to hear him clearly confirm my fear. Kenneth Frederick Fuller lost his life to suicide on October 6, 2007. I still struggle with thinking and rationalizing what went wrong and what could have been different. But one thing is for sure: my grief with Kenny was that too much remained. I lost control of my speech at his funeral when I was asked to stand up and give a few words. I couldn't stop sobbing and crying because I knew he had more in him to give, to become, and now his wife would be a widow, his five children fatherless.

One of the best quotes I have ever heard of that defines my obsession with people's potential is by the late Dr. Myles Munroe:

> The wealthiest place in the world is not the gold mines of South America or the oil fields of Iraq or Iran. They are not the diamond mines of South Africa or the banks of the world. The wealthiest place on the planet is just down the road. It is the cemetery. There lie buried companies that were never started, inventions that were never made, bestselling books that were never written, and masterpieces that were never painted. In the cemetery is buried the greatest treasure of untapped potential.
> **—Myles Munroe**

Not by Luck

Imagine showing up on the first day for track and field of the 2024 Olympics. You're excited to see the activity while sitting in the crowd, and then, out of the blue, you hear your name over the intercom systems. A little shocked, you rush out of the stands and into the field office, where you are equally surprised to see your high school track coach. They bring you over to the desk and inform you that one of the high jumpers slated to participate for your country has pulled out for personal reasons.

Your high school coach has recommended that you replace them so that your country can have a chance to win gold. The logic is that if a person competes, there is a better chance of winning than if we forfeit. In this scenario, let's say you accept and go out to the field and begin to compare yourself to these world-class athletes who have committed and considered every action they have taken for the past several years in terms of how that action will impact their ability to thrive in this moment. You, on the other hand, although you possess some natural talent, have not developed in a way that would win anything outside of a footrace at your company's annual cookout.

This silly anecdote illustrates a point that you cannot compete with world-class athletes simply by trying: you must train. Training requires commitment far beyond what makes us comfortable. As Darren Hardy says, "Commitment is doing the thing you said you were going to do long after the mood you said it in has left you." If we are going to succeed in any endeavor, we must learn how to remain. The amazing irony is that many people are sitting in the stands as spectators and waiting on something miraculous to happen that will allow them the opportunity to win. They are, I suppose, waiting to win the lottery of life, providing minimum effort while expecting maximum gain. When you look over their daily habits, they are doing nothing to train to be the absolute best and to become the person who has the capacity to win.

There is a pattern of what it takes to win in sports, business, and life. This pattern is putting in the right mile markers that allow you to grow in such a way that you become the person who wins. Many people have the false assumption that all they need to do is the right thing, and they will get recognized and rewarded, but that's not the way life works. We don't get lucky and win; we become good, and that empowers us to have the ability to win. Every once in a while, someone hits a lucky home run, hits a lucky shot, or even gets a hole in one. None of these isolated moments makes a champion. That person who has fifteen minutes of fame barely stands out. It takes a commitment and entering a process of becoming for any person in any endeavor to have the ability to remain relevant.

Betty White, with more than eighty years on the silver screen, has enjoyed the longest active career in the public eye of anyone on the planet. Between Betty and the queen of England, you question who has the most grit. She is a symbol to many as a sign of longevity and endurance. In a world where so many people change jobs almost every year and switch industries every other year, I have to question how someone could ever become good at anything—let alone great.

> I had no idea that I would still be around at this point for one thing, but that I'd still be privileged enough to still be in this business. And it is such a privilege. And the bottom line I think to the television business is that unless you're a real bad egg, it is such fun. It really is. Thank you, thank you from the bottom of my heart.[1]
> **—Betty White**

Quitting has become so easy. Statistics say that 30 percent of the workforce will change jobs every twelve months, which means people are quitting before they even learn how to become good at something.[2] This same study suggested that the average person will change careers (not jobs) five to seven times within their lifetime.

One of the most significant research areas in the field of personal success has been that of grit. Both Angela Duckworth and the coauthors Linda Kaplan Thaler and Robin Koval have contributed significantly to the work of understanding the secret ingredient that separates high achievers from average people.

Kaplan Thaler and Koval describe grit as *guts, resilience, initiative,* and *tenacity.* In *Grit to Great,* they describe how successful people have the guts to acknowledge their current level of skill without giving up hope that they can be the best.[3] These individuals and teams also have the resilience to bounce back and develop a comfort with failing without conceding to failure. Super achievers take initiative and demonstrate the ability to insist that being proactive is much more powerful. Finally, gritty people have the relentless tenacity that ensures they will win.

For You to Remain Relevant, You Must First Remain

I was never really one to be impressed with celebrities. As a young man and student of history, I noticed that people who were incredibly influential in one generation and place in the world were almost unknown in another. I was shocked on a visit to Guatemala during graduate school that no one knew who Dr. Martin Luther King Jr. was. At first, I was discouraged that someone so prominent and central to American life was completely unknown less than 1,200 miles away. I thought, *What could I do of any significance that could make a difference within my own community, city, nation, or generation? Was there any endeavor that I could pursue to demonstrate that my time on earth mattered?*

I began to notice that those who were making a difference beyond their industry, nation, and generational boundaries all had a similar trait that proves difficult for most people. This trait was that they were only known for one thing. Ben Franklin practically created the insurance, health care, and banking industries. Yet for all his prowess as an inventor, writer, printer, and activist, Franklin was committed to the founding of the United States, and he is known as a founding father of this country. The pattern is quite clear that if you choose to keep experimenting with a bunch of things, you will find yourself unable to emerge with the one thing. In *City Slickers*, Curly holds up his one finger and educates these "city boys" that everyone has to discover their one thing.

My son has taken up Tae Kwon Do and is constantly frustrated about staying on his belt level, mainly due to the infrequency of class attendance. It's cute when he comes to my office to try to take my black belt from me so that he can call himself a black belt. I studied Kenpo Karate under Master Fines Whitley, one of the greats in that discipline. With late nights, lots of sweat, and intense katas and sparring, I earned a rank. What my son doesn't seem to understand is that the black belt is not the achievement; it's simply the recognition of the achievement. To a person who didn't earn it, the black belt is simply a piece of cloth. The same can be said of diplomas, certifications, and professional licenses. I have heard of people who cheat to get the grade or pass the exam, not realizing that the paper has no value without the price. The honor is in the work of becoming.

It Starts with Vision

One of my mentors, Paul Martinelli, has a calling card whenever he signs off on an email or a call: he challenges you to hold your image. As a high school dropout who has built several companies doing more than half a billion dollars in revenue, he understands the importance of changing the narrative and the stories we tell ourselves about who we are and who we can become. The picture you hold dominates everything about the direction your life turns. Your eyeballs sit right below the prefrontal cortex of your brain, and there are powerful connections through every major component of this precious organ. The visual cortex is probably one of the most unifying elements of our learning. Even those who are born without sight are often gifted with enhanced abilities of perception that give them a heightened awareness to envision concepts of the future.

As mentioned in the "Recreate" chapter, it is imperative to be reminded that we are constantly creating our world with the dominant image that we hold in our mind. The projection of our images is often revealed in our words, and we could say that we design our worlds with our words. So, whatever picture or image you allow to dominate your mind will indeed create your reality. This is good news! This means that the moment you decide what you want, what you really want, you can immediately change your life. Now, it's not about creating a vision board with the perfect body, car, and house, viewing it one time a day, and expecting things to be different. This is about focusing on one idea so powerful that it becomes emotionally irresistible. To give space for the idea to be formed, born, and nurtured into a burning desire. Napoleon Hill suggests that most people's ideas are stillborn and need the breath of life injected in them with definite plans and immediate action.[5] So, if you are going to remain, what are you going to do to hold your image?

> No one can resist an idea whose time has come.
> —Victor Hugo

Driven by Purpose

When I began the journey of writing this book more than fifteen years ago, I really believed that something in me was defective because I wasn't defective enough. It seemed that every one of the people I was reading about had a horrible past with insurmountable odds, and I was simply a normal person. Nick Vujicic is a tremendous speaker from Australia who has traveled the world many times over because he inspires people to live without limits. Now, if you have seen him speak, you already know that he was born without arms and legs. In many countries, they would have done a same-day abortion because they would have predetermined that he could add no value to the world. Now he is one of the most sought-after keynote speakers in the world. So, imagine me in April 2006, sitting there in Barnes & Noble and feeling sorry for myself because I can't be an internationally sought-after speaker because I have both my arms and legs.

The imposter syndrome and the victim mentality are two sides of the same coin, creating a ridiculous narrative that tends to stop us from living out our purpose. We obsessively look for reasons to count ourselves out, which is why we are often so impressed with anyone who holds themselves in high esteem. But wait, if you follow them into their bedroom and wait until they turn out the lights, they get to lie there looking at the ceiling living with the same doubts: "Am I good enough? Do I deserve it? What makes me so different?"

I believe it's critical to go back to the axiom Be x Do = Have. Everything you have is a direct consequence of what you do. Sometimes we get lucky, and other times, we experience things that don't go our way, but life is rarely defined by the anomalies; it is revealed by its consistencies. James Allen wrote, "Circumstance does not make the man; it reveals him to himself." Our results are an overflow of our actions, but our actions are inextricably linked to our beliefs. The entirety of our character is not the sum total of who we are, but the choices we make, observed over time, reveal the truth of what we truly believe.

To live on purpose, you must believe in purpose. Now, I am not here to debate philosophy with anyone; that would not serve anyone. I do not believe faith is a weapon used to battle ideas. I believe faith is a shield designed to protect me, and if I use it as a weapon, I do severe damage to myself and my faith. So, I reserve the right to my beliefs. I believe in an intelligently ordered universe, I believe love is the highest calling, and I believe that life has purpose. These beliefs, if they are truly believed, create an obligation to suspend self-doubt and embrace the fact that my life is not an accident—and that I have a duty to discover and reveal the purpose for which I am here. I am not suggesting that everyone needs to believe what I believe, but if there is no foundational belief that drives you forward, it is unlikely you will press through when things get tough.

Defined by Character

One of my clients was recently abandoned by her husband, who happens to be a very charismatic and influential person within the community of speakers and coaches. He had internal character issues concerning fidelity that she would begin to challenge him on, and he didn't like being challenged, so he left. Well, this client went into a really dark place, and her business began to suffer. I became very concerned that her business might not make it if she stayed disconnected for too long. Three months later, I was surprised when she popped out of her shell and came out ready to get to work. I asked how she was able to be so strong when she felt her life had been ripped apart, and she simply explained that she had done it her entire life.

As a teenager, she escaped from an abusive relationship in Mexico and crossed the border into the United States with her son. Since she needed to make money, she would make jewelry all night and set up a table at the local mall to sell it. She began hiring people to sell her jewelry and eventually earned enough to open her own jewelry store in the mall. Eventually, someone asked if they could rent a small corner in her store to sell cell phones. Remembering her beginnings, she allowed them to do just that. She noticed that with a small cell phone stand, they were making more than she was with much less effort. She figured out how to open up her own cell phone store, which led to more than seven locations.

Meanwhile, she suffered in abusive relationships both physically and mentally, and she wrestled with depression and even thoughts of suicide. It was then that she opened her heart to a charming guy, and they fell madly in love. So, when he left her, it was a pain she had never experienced before. Out of the ashes of that pain, she has begun creating a massive organization that speaks to the hearts of Latina women who feel trapped in silence and need to hear the power of their own voices. This is what character does. It causes us to go deeper inside ourselves and find out there is still more we have to give than could ever be taken from us. I am grateful this client has allowed me to share her story, although she is not yet ready to share her name. She is not alone. What determines our ability to ultimately achieve what we set out to do in life is discovering whether we will keep standing in the storm, in the trial, and not when conditions are nice. It is human nature to assume the best of ourselves when conditions are perfect, but that's not where life is lived. We live in the arena of chaos and destruction, and if we hold fast, we will emerge victorious.

This is What It Means to Remain

Time teaches all things to those who live forever, but I have not the luxury of eternity. Yet, within my allotted time I must practice the art of patience for nature acts never in haste. To create the olive, king of all trees, a hundred years is required. An onion plant is old in nine weeks. I have lived as an onion plant. It has not pleased me. Now I wouldst become the greatest of olive trees and in truth the greatest _____.
—Og Mandino[5]

You can fill in that blank. This is why I believe the resilient will always beat the intelligent. I want to challenge you to learn more about what you do until you are doing all you know.

God bless!

REFERENCES

Introduction

Soren Kierkegaard, Goodreads, accessed March 11, 2021, https://www.goodreads.com/quotes/423155-now-with-god-s-help-i-shall-become-myself.

Earl Nightingale, BrainyQuote, accessed March 11, 2021, https://www.brainyquote.com/quotes/earl_nightingale_159030.

Quoted in "13 Martin Luther King Jr Quotes on Education that YOU Need to Know!" Our Luther King, accessed March 11, 2021, https://ourlutherking.com/martin-luther-king-jr-quotes-on-education.

Quoted in Joel Brown, "50 Inspirational Myles Munroe Quotes to Fire You Up," Addicted2Success, accessed March 11, 2021, https://addicted2success.com/quotes/50-inspirational-myles-munroe-quotes-to-fire-you-up

"Stanford Marshmallow Experiment," Wikipedia, accessed March 11, 2021, https://en.wikipedia.org/wiki/Stanford_marshmallow_experiment.

Benjamin Disraeli, Quotes.net, accessed March 11, 2021, https://www.quotes.net/quote/2962

Quoted in "84 Motivational Quotes by James Allen for Your Soul, Heart and Mind," TheFamousPeople, accessed March 11, 2021, https://quotes.thefamouspeople.com/james-allen-1724.php

Robert C. Barkman, "See the World Through Patterns," *Psychology Today*, accessed March 11, 2021, https://www.psychologytoday.com/us/blog/singular-perspective/201801/see-the-world-through-patterns

Lee Iacocca and William Novak, *Iacocca: An Autobiography*, read by Lee Iacocca (Random House Audio, 2007), Audible audio ed.

Jim Collins, Good to Great: Why Some Companies Make the Leap and Others Don't, read by Jim Collins (HarperAudio, 2005), Audible audio ed.

Napoleon Hill, Think and Grow Rich, read by Napoleon Hill Foundation (Nightingale-Conant, 1993), Audible audio ed.

"Practical Tips for School Leaders #38," St. John's County School District, August 10, 2020, accessed March 22, 2021, https://www.stjohns.k12. fl.us/leadership/wp-content/uploads/sites/77/2020/08/Leadershi p-Development-Tip-38-The-Law-of-Empowerment.pdf

John C. Maxwell, The 21 Irrefutable Laws of Leadership, read by Henry O. Arnold (HarperCollins Leadership, 2020).

Joseph Grenny, Kerry Patterson, David Maxfield, Ron McMillan, and Al Switzler, Influencer: The New Science of Leading Change, 2nd ed. (New York: McGraw Hill Education, 2013), 6.

George Santayana, Goodreads, accessed April 21, 2021, https://www.go-odreads.com/quotes/634544-those-who-cannot-remember-the-pas t-are-condemned-to-repeat

Chapter 1

John C. Maxwell, Winning with People, read by Henry O. Arnold (HarperCollins, 2020), Audible ed.

Maxwell, Winning with People.

Maxwell, Winning with People.

Bruce Lipton, The Biology of Belief, read by Bruce Lipton (Sounds True, 2006), Audible ed.

Lipton, The Biology of Belief.

Lipton, The Biology of Belief.

Lipton, The Biology of Belief.

Lipton, The Biology of Belief.

Lipton, The Biology of Belief.

Maxwell Maltz and Dan Kennedy, The New Psycho-Cybernetics: A Mind Technology for Living Your Life Without Limits, read by Maxwell Maltz and Dan Kennedy (Nightingale-Conant, 1998), Audible ed.

Lipton, The Biology of Belief.

David Rock, Quiet Leadership: Six Steps to Transforming Performance at Work, read by Pete Larkin (HarperAudio, 2011), Audible ed.

Lipton, The Biology of Belief.

Lipton, The Biology of Belief.

Lipton, The Biology of Belief.

Marcus Buckingham, StandOut: The Groundbreaking New Strengths Assessment from the Leader of the Strengths Revolution, read by Kelly Ryan Dolan (Oasis, 2011), Audible ed.

Earl Nightingale, "The Strangest Secret," Nightingale-Conant, accessed April 21, 2021, https://www.nightingale.com/articles/the-strangest-secret/

"Lincoln's 'Failures'?" Abraham Lincoln Online, 2018, accessed February 2, 2021, http://www.abrahamlincolnonline.org/lincoln/education/failures.htm

Wikipedia, "Phillis Wheatley," last modified March 6, 2021, accessed March 12, 2021, https://en.wikipedia.org/wiki/Phillis_Wheatley

"Edison's Failed Inventions," Library of Congress, accessed February 2, 2021, http://www.americaslibrary.gov/aa/edison/aa_edison_fail_3.html

Harriet Tubman, PBS Black Culture Connection, accessed February 2, 2021, https://www.pbs.org/black-culture/explore/harriet-tubman/

John C. Maxwell, Failing Forward: Turning Mistakes into Stepping Stones for Success, read by Henry O. Arnold (HarperCollins, 2020), Audible ed.

Michael Behe, Darwin's Black Box: The Biochemical Challenge to Evolution, read by Marc William (Tantor Audio, 2019), Audible ed.

Dallas Willard, Renovation of the Heart: Putting On the Character of Christ, read by Dallas Willard (christianaudio.com, 2002), Audible ed.

Steven Carr Reuben, "What Baby Elephants Can Teach Us about Human Freedom," Huffington Post, March 13, 2013, accessed March 12, 2021, https://www.huffpost.com/entry/what-baby-elephants-can-teach-us-about-human-freedom_b_2452099

John C. Maxwell, Developing the Leader Within You (Nashville: Thomas Nelson Inc., 1993), 81.

Chapter 2

J. Robert Clinton, The Making of a Leader: Recognizing the Lessons and Stages of Leadership Development, read by Charles Constant (Two Words Publishing, 2017), Audible ed.

Diana Chapman, Jim Dethmer, and Kaley Klemp, The 15 Commitments of Conscious Leadership: A New Paradigm for Sustainable Success, read by Jim Dethmer (Dethmer, Chapman, and Klemp, 2014), Audible ed.

David Guy Powers, How to Say a Few Words (Garden City, NY: Doubleday, 1953), 109.

Andy Stanley, The Principle of the Path: How to Get from Where You Are to Where You Want to Be, read by John Gauger (Oasis Audio, 2009), Audible ed.

Chapter 3

Recognize," Oxford Languages, accessed February 16, 2021, https://www.google.com/search?q=recognize+definition

William James, "The Energies of Men" (1907), Classics in the History of Psychology, accessed March 22, 2021, http://psychclassics.yorku.ca/James/energies.htm

Andy Rooney, "I've Learned," edited by Mike Snyder, accessed March 16, 2021, http://kubik.org/lighter/rooney.htm

Stephen R. Covey, The 7 Habits of Highly Effective People: Powerful Lessons in Personal Change, read by Stephen R. Covey (Simon & Schuster Audio, 2004), Audible ed.

David Allen, Getting Things Done: The Art of Stress-Free Productivity, read by David Allen (Simon & Schuster Audio, 2001), Audible ed.

David Rock, Your Brain at Work: Strategies for Overcoming Distraction, Regaining Focus, and Working Smarter All Day Long, read by Bob Walter (HarperAudio, 2011), Audible ed.

Bruce Lipton, The Biology of Belief, read by Bruce Lipton (Sounds True, 2006), Audible ed.

Quoted in Gregg Fauceglia, "Men Simply Don't Think," Medium, February 16, 2020, accessed March 16, 2021, https://medium.com/@greggfauceglia/men-simply-dont-think-73c3d2d0d332

A. A. Milne, The House at Pooh Corner (New York: Dutton Children's Books, 1992), 16.

Quoted in Erika Andersen, "21 Quotes by Henry Ford on Business, Leadership, and Life," Forbes, May 13, 2013, accessed March 16, 2021, https://www.forbes.com/sites/erikaandersen/2013/05/31/21-quotes-from-henry-ford-on-business-leadership-and-life/?sh=2ad455f5293c

Napoleon Hill, Think and Grow Rich, read by Napoleon Hill Foundation (Nightingale-Conant, 1993), Audible ed.

Diana Chapman, Jim Dethmer, and Kaley Klemp, The 15 Commitments of Conscious Leadership: A New Paradigm for Sustainable Success, read by Jim Dethmer (Dethmer, Chapman, and Klemp, 2014), Audible ed.

Mihaly Csikszentmihalyi, Flow: Living at the Peak of Your Abilities, read by Mihaly Csikszentmihalyi (Nightingale-Conant, 1994), Audible ed.

Adobe Stock image, accessed March 9, 2021, https://stock.adobe.com/search?k=bell+curve

Martin Luther King, Jr., "Beyond Vietnam," New York City, April 4, 1967, accessed March 16, 2021, https://kinginstitute.stanford.edu/king-papers/documents/beyond-vietnam

Ronald Reagan, "Presidential First Inaugural Address," Washington, D.C., January 20, 1981, accessed March 16, 2021, https://avalon.law.yale.edu/20th_century/reagan1.asp

Chapter 4

Refuse," Oxford Languages, accessed February 16, 2021, https://www.google.com/search?q=refuse+definition

James Allen, As a Man Thinketh, read by Brian Holsopple (Thinking Stuff, 2007), Audible ed.

T.S. Eliot, Forbes Quotes, accessed March 16, 2021, https://www.forbes.com/quotes/8887/

Stephen R. Covey, A. Roger Merrill, and Rebecca R. Merrill, First Things First: To Live, to Love, to Learn, to Leave a Legacy (New York: Free Press, 1994), 59.

Stephen R. Covey, The 7 Habits of Highly Effective People: Powerful Lessons in Personal Change, read by Stephen R. Covey (Simon & Schuster, 2004), Audible ed.

Kendra Cherry, "How Experience Changes Brain Plasticity," VeryWellMind, February 3, 2021, accessed March 23, 2021, https://www.verywellmind.com/what-is-brain-plasticity-2794886

"Positive-Negative Asymmetry," iResearchnet, accessed March 23, 2021, https://psychology.iresearchnet.com/social-psychology/social-cognition/positive-negative-asymmetry/

David Rock, Your Brain at Work: Strategies for Overcoming Distraction, Regaining Focus, and Working Smarter All Day Long, read by Bob Walter (HarperAudio, 2011), Audible ed.

Bruce Wilkinson, The Dream Giver: Following Your God-Given Destiny, read by Bruce Wilkinson (Mission Audio, 2015), Audible ed.

Quoted in "31 Excuses Quotes about Those Who Always Make Excuses," Spirit Button, February 3, 2018, accessed March 23, 2021, https://www.spiritbutton.com/excuses-quotes/

Proverbs 27:26, King James Version, accessed March 15, 2021, https://my.bible.com/bible/1/PRO.27.KJV

John C. Maxwell, BrainyQuote, accessed March 23, 2021, https://www.brainyquote.com/quotes/john_c_maxwell_600865

Andy Stanley, Quotemaster, accessed March 16, 2021, https://www.quotemaster.org/qd6a88a932d87a6e717e4cdcb43919504

Willard, Dallas, Renovation of the Heart: Putting On the Character of Christ, read by Dallas Willard (christianaudio.com, 2002), Audible ed.

John C. Maxwell, speech given at the World Marriott Hotel, Orlando, FL, March 2019.

Quoted in Maria Popova, "Henry David Thoreau on Defining Your Success," July 12, 2012, accessed March 16, 2021, https://www.theatlantic.com/entertainment/archive/2012/07/henry-david-thoreau-on-defining-your-own-success/259730/

Forrest Gump, directed by Robert Zemeckis, Paramount Pictures, 1994.

Forrest Gump.

Luke 8:51-56, King James Version, accessed February 16, 2021, https://my.bible.com/bible/1/LUK.8.KJV

Chapter 5

Resolve," Oxford Languages, accessed March 16, 2021, https://www.google.com/search?q=resolve+definition

Denis Waitley, BrainyQuote, accessed March 23, 2021, https://www.brainyquote.com/quotes/denis_waitley_146913?src=t_resolve

Napoleon Hill, Think and Grow Rich, read by Napoleon Hill Foundation (Nightingale-Conant, 1993), Audible ed.

Ambrose Bierce, BrainyQuote, accessed March 17, 2021, https://www.brainyquote.com/quotes/ambrose_bierce_117978

Hill, Think and Grow Rich.

Zig Ziglar, Quotefancy, accessed March 17, 2021, https://quotefancy.com/quote/943274/Zig-Ziglar

Hill, Think and Grow Rich.

Quoted in Jake Carlson, "People Don't Fail Because They Aim Too High," Family Before Fortune, May 26, 2015, accessed March 17, 2021, http://www.familybeforefortune.com/blog/people-dont-fail-because-the y-aim-too-high/

Paul R. Scheele, Natural Brilliance: Overcome Any Challenge ... At Will, 2nd ed. (Minnetonka, MN: Learning Strategies Corporation, 2000), 6-8, accessed March 23, 2021, https://www.learningstrategies.com/resources/prfest/pdf/Natural-Brilliance-Book.pdf

Hill, Think and Grow Rich.

William Pollard, BrainyQuotes, accessed March 23, 2021, https://www.brainyquote.com/quotes/william_pollard_163253

Andy Stanley, Visioneering: God's Blueprint for Developing and Maintaining Vision, read by Lloyd James (christianaudio.com), Audible ed.

Quoted in Kristy J. O'Hara, "John C. Maxwell Partners with World Vision," January 21, 2016, accessed April 21, 2021, https://www.worldvision.org/christian-faith-news-stories/john-c-maxwell-partners-world-vision

Bill Clinton, "1998 State of the Union Address," Washington, D.C., January 27, 1998, The Washington Post (speech transcript), accessed March 17, 2021, https://www.washingtonpost.com/wp-srv/politics/special/states/docs/sou98.htm

Marc Rosenberg, "Marc My Words: The Coming Knowledge Tsunami," Learning Solutions, October 10, 2017, accessed March 17, 2021, https://learningsolutionsmag.com/articles/2468/marc-my-words-the-comin g-knowledge-tsunami

Bruce Lee, BrainyQuote, accessed March 17, 2021, https://www.brainy-quote.com/quotes/bruce_lee_413509

Nathan Nolan, "Memento Mori," Esquire, January 29, 2007, accessed March 17, 2021, https://www.esquire.com/entertainment/books/a1564/memento-mori-0301/

James Allen, Goodreads, accessed March 17, 2021, https://www.goodreads.com/quotes/7318335-only-by-much-searching-and-mining-are-gold-and-diamonds

Jonathan Haidt, The Happiness Hypothesis: Finding Modern Truth in Ancient Wisdom, read by Ryan Vincent Anderson (Hachette Audio, 2018), Audible ed.

David Rock, Your Brain at Work: Strategies for Overcoming Distraction, Regaining Focus, and Working Smarter All Day Long, read by Roger Wayne (HarperAudio, 2020), Audible ed.

Rock, Your Brain at Work.

"The Gut-Brain Connection," Harvard Health Publishing, January 21, 2020, accessed March 17, 2021, https://www.health.harvard.edu/diseases-and-conditions/the-gut-brain-connection

Chip Heath and Dan Heath, Switch: How to Change Things When Change Is Hard, read by Charles Kahlenberg (Random House Audio, 2010), Audible ed.

Daniel H. Pink, Drive: The Surprising Truth About What Motivates Us, read by Daniel H. Pink (Penguin Audio, 2009), Audible ed.

Daniel Goleman, Emotional Intelligence: Why It Can Matter More than IQ, 10th anniversary ed. (New York: Bantam, 2012), 18.

Andy Stanley, Goodreads, accessed March 18, 2021, https://www.goodreads.com/quotes/556851-direction-not-intention-determines-your-destination

Proverbs 29:18, American Standard Version, accessed March 17, 2021, https://www.bible.com/bible/compare/PRO.29.18

Chapter 6

Release," Oxford Languages, accessed March 23, 2021, https://www.google.com/search?q=release+definition

Dorothy Day, Goodreads, accessed March 18, 2021, https://www.goodreads.com/quotes/1286525-the-best-things-to-do-with-the-best-things-in

John C. Maxwell, QuoteTab, accessed March 23, 2021, https://www.quotetab.com/quote/by-john-c-maxwell/be-a-river-not-a-reservoir

Larry Crabb, AZ Quotes, accessed March 23, 2021, https://www.azquotes.com/quote/726264

Gregory Boyd, "The Risk of Love and the Source of Evil," ReKnew, August 26, 2014, accessed March 23, 2021, https://reknew.org/2014/08/the-risk-of-love-the-source-of-evil/

John Blakey, "Stephen Covey, Interdependence and the Deeper Facts," Challenging Coaching, accessed March 23, 2021, https://challenging-coaching.co.uk/stephen-covey-interdependence-the-deeper-facts/

Kendra Cherry, "The 5 Levels of Maslow's Hierarchy of Needs," VeryWellMind, March 19, 2021, accessed March 23, 2021, https://www.verywellmind.com/what-is-maslows-hierarchy-of-needs-4136760

Eric Hoffer, Goodreads, accessed March 23, 2021, https://www.goodreads.com/quotes/339378-no-matter-what-our-achievements-might-be-we-think-well

Daniel Goleman, Social Intelligence: The New Science of Human Relationships, read by Dennis Boutsikaris (Macmillan Audio, 2006), Audible ed.

Adam Grant, Give and Take: A Revolutionary Approach to Success, read by Brian Keith Lewis (Penguin Audio, 2013), Audible ed.

Hernandez, Michael, "The Property Laws of a Toddler," Sermon Search, accessed March 19, 2021, https://www.sermonsearch.com/sermon-illustrations/710/property-laws-of-a-toddler/

"Study: It Pays to be Generous," The Ascent, November 7, 2019, accessed March 23, 2021, https://www.fool.com/the-ascent/research/study-it-pays-be-generous

Gretchen Rubin, The Happiness Project, read by Gretchen Rubin (HarperAudio, 2009), Audible ed.

Brené Brown, The Gifts of Imperfection, 10th anniversary ed., read by Brené Brown (Random House Audio, 2020), Audible ed.

Friedrich Nietzsche, Goodreads, accessed March 23, 2021, https://www.goodreads.com/quotes/165589-this-is-the-hardest-of-all-to-close-the-open

Chapter 7

Recreate," Oxford Languages, accessed February 17, 2021, https://www.google.com/search?q=recreate+definition

Roy T. Bennett, Goodreads, accessed March 20, 2021, https://www.goodreads.com/quotes/7858744-attitude-is-a-choice-happiness-is-a-choice-optimism-is

Napoleon Hill, BrainyQuote, accessed March 30, 2021, https://www.brainyquote.com/quotes/napoleon_hill_152856

Marianne Williamson, "Our Deepest Fear," Personal Growth Courses, accessed March 23, 2021, https://www.personalgrowthcourses.net/stories/williamson.ourdeepestfear.invitation

John C. Maxwell, Developing the Leader within You (Nashville: Thomas Nelson, 1993), 31.

James Allen, Goodreads, accessed March 24, 2021, https://www.goodreads.com/quotes/7728269-the-soul-attracts-that-which-it-secretly-harbors-that-which

Thomas Troward, The Hidden Power (New York: Robert M. McBride & Company, 1921), 13.

David Rock, Your Brain at Work: Strategies for Overcoming Distraction, Regaining Focus, and Working Smarter All Day Long, read by Roger Wayne (HarperAudio, 2020), Audible ed.

The Matrix, directed by Lilly Wachowski and Lana Wachowski, Warner Bros., 1999.

Troward, The Hidden Power, 13.

Bruce Lipton, "The Wisdom of Your Cells," Bruce H. Lipton, PhD, June 7, 2012, accessed March 23, 2021, https://www.brucelipton.com/resource/article/the-wisdom-your-cells

Lipton, "The Wisdom of Your Cells."

"Ruah," Wikipedia, last modified March 14, 2021, https://en.wikipedia.org/wiki/Ruah

"Inspire," Online Etymology Dictionary, accessed February 23, 2021, www.etymonline.com/word/inspiration

Thomas Troward, The Creative Process in the Individual, Law of Attraction Haven, accessed March 24, 2021, https://www.law-of-attraction-haven.com/support-files/the-creative-process-in-the-individual-thomas-troward.pdf

Wallace D. Wattles, "One Original Formless Stuff," Wallace D. Wattles, December 11, 2013, accessed March 24, 2021, https://www.wallaced-wattles.org/2013/12/11/one-original-formless-stuff

"Cortical Remapping," Wikipedia, last modified April 17, 2020, https://en.wikipedia.org/wiki/Cortical_remapping

Hal Elrod, The Miracle Morning: The Not-So-Obvious Secret Guaranteed to Transform Your Life Before 8AM, read by Rob Actis (Hal Elrod, 2013), Audible ed.

Chapter 8

Rejoice," Oxford Languages, accessed March 16, 2021, https://www.google.com/search?q=rejoice+definition

Nelson Mandela, BrainyQuote, accessed March 16, 2021, https://www.
brainyquote.com/quotes/nelson_mandela_393048

J.D. Roth, "Your Money: The Missing Manual," O'Reilly, accessed
March 23, 2021, https://www.oreilly.com/library/view/your-money-
the/9780596809430/ch01.html

Grant Suneson, "These Are the 25 Richest Countries in the World," USA
Today, July 8, 2019, accessed March 23, 2021, https://www.usatoday.com/
story/money/2019/07/07/richest-countries-in-the-world/39630693/

Laura Begley Bloom, "The 20 Happiest Countries in the World in 2021 (Guess
Where the U.S. Ranked?)," Forbes, March 19, 2021, accessed March 23,
2021, https://www.forbes.com/sites/laurabegleybloom/2021/03/19/th
e-20-happiest-countries-in-the-world-in-2021/?sh=716b04cd70a0

Zig Ziglar, internetPoem, accessed March 16, 2021, https://internet-
poem.com/zig-ziglar/quotes/money-won-t-make-you-happy-bu
t-everybody-wants-to-47002/10/

Stephen R. Covey, The 7 Habits of Highly Effective People: Powerful
Lessons in Personal Change, read by Stephen R. Covey (Simon &
Schuster Audio, 2004), Audible ed.

John Ortberg, The Life You've Always Wanted: Spiritual Discipline for
Ordinary People, read by Jay Charles (Zondervan, 2002), Audible ed.

Theodore Roosevelt, Goodreads, accessed March 19, 2021, https://www.
goodreads.com/quotes/7-it-is-not-the-critic-who-counts-not-the-man

"48 Famous Failures Who Will Inspire You to Achieve," Wanderlust Worker,
accessed April 2, 2021, https://www.wanderlustworker.com/48-famou
s-failures-who-will-inspire-you-to-achieve/#colonelharlandsanders

Angela Duckworth, Grit: The Power of Passion and Perseverance, read by
Angela Duckworth (Simon & Schuster Audio, 2016), Audible ed.

The Diary of Anne Frank, directed by George Stevens, Twentieth Century
Fox, 1959.

Proverbs 24:10, New International Version, accessed February 24, 2021,
https://biblehub.com/proverbs/24-10.htm

Chapter 9

Reengage," Dictionary.com, accessed March 22, 2021, https://www.dictio-
nary.com/browse/reengage

Nathan Nolan, "Memento Mori," Esquire, January 29, 2007, accessed March 17, 2021, https://www.esquire.com/entertainment/books/a1564/memento-mori-0301/

Kathryn Sanford, "30 Powerful Success and Failure Quotes that Will Lead You to Success," Lifehack, accessed March 20, 2021, https://www.lifehack.org/articles/communication/30-quotes-failure-that-will-lead-you-success.html

Nelson Mandela, Goodreads, accessed March 20, 2021, https://www.goodreads.com/quotes/270163-do-not-judge-me-by-my-successes-judge-me-by

Andy Stanley, Momentum, YouTube, July 24, 2016, accessed April 5, 2021, https://www.youtube.com/watch?v=R2NMx4mrxfY&t=621s

Jim Collins, "A Culture of Discipline," Jim Collins, accessed March 20, 2021, https://www.jimcollins.com/concepts/a-culture-of-discipline.html

Les Brown, "Why It Pays to be Hungry," YouTube, accessed March 23, 2021, https://www.youtube.com/watch?v=xFr0FKnaLDk

Maya Angelou, Goodreads, accessed April 21, 2021, https://www.goodreads.com/quotes/228308-you-may-not-control-all-the-events-that-happen-to

Bonnie St. John and Allen P. Haines, Micro-Resilience: Minor Shifts for Major Boosts in Focus, Drive, and Energy, read by Bonnie St. John and Allen P. Haines (Hachette Audio, 2017), Audible ed.

David McCasland, Eric Liddell: Pure Gold (Grand Rapids: Discovery House Publishers, 2001), 48-51.

Zig Ziglar, AZQuotes, accessed April 21, 2021, https://www.azquotes.com/quote/521447

John C. Maxwell, Developing the Leader within You (Nashville: Thomas Nelson, 1993), 80-81.

Tim S. Grover and Shari Wenk, Relentless: From Good to Great to Unstoppable, read by Pete Simonelli (Simon and Schuster Audio, 2020), Audible ed.

Grover and Wenk, Relentless.

St. John and Haines, Micro-Resilience.

Mihaly Csikszentmihalyi, Flow: Living at the Peak of Your Abilities, read by Mihaly Csikszentmihalyi (Nightingale Conant, 1994), Audible ed.

Chapter 10

Refine," Oxford Languages, accessed March 20, 2021, https://www.google.
com/search?q=refine+definition

Benjamin Franklin, Goodreads, accessed March 24, 2021, https://www.go-
odreads.com/quotes/103000-without-continual-growth-and-progres
s-such-words-as-improvement-achievement

James Allen, BrainyQuote, accessed March 24, 2021, https://www.brainy-
quote.com/quotes/james_lane_allen_194690

Michael E. Gerber, The E-Myth Revisited: Why Most Small Businesses
Don't Work and What to Do About It, read by Michael E. Gerber,
(HarperAudio, 2004), Audible ed.

Helmut Schmidt, BrainyQuote, accessed March 24, 2021, https://www.
brainyquote.com/quotes/helmut_schmidt_756166

Maya Angelou, BrainyQuote, accessed March 24, 2021, https://www.
brainyquote.com/quotes/maya_angelou_132625

Jeff Olson, The Slight Edge: Turning Simple Disciplines into Massive
Success and Happiness (Austin: Greenleaf Book Group Press, 2013).

Kyle Hoffman, "41 Gym Membership Statistics that Will Surprise You,"
Noobgains, March 27, 2020, accessed March 24, 2021, https://noob-
gains.com/gym-membership-statistics/

"The $72 Billion Weight Loss and Diet Control Market in the United
States," Business Wire, February 25, 2019, accessed March 24, 2021,
https://www.businesswire.com/news/home/20190225005455/en/

Vince Lombardi, Jr., Goodreads, accessed March 24, 2021, https://www.
goodreads.com/quotes/392543-perfection-is-not-attainable-but-if-we-
chase-perfection-we

Napoleon Hill, "Napoleon Hill Quotes," BrainyQuote, accessed March
24, 2021, https://www.brainyquote.com/quotes/napoleon_hill_152853

Simon Sinek, The Infinite Game, read by Simon Sinek (Penguin Audio,
2018), Audible ed.

Sinek, The Infinite Game.

H. James Harrington, Goodreads, accessed March 24, 2021, https://
www.goodreads.com/quotes/632992-measurement-is-the-first-step
-that-leads-to-control-and

Olson, The Slight Edge, 81-83.

John C. Maxwell, Today Matters: 12 Daily Practices to Guarantee Tomorrow's Success, read by John C. Maxwell (Hachette Audio, 2004), Audible ed.

John C. Maxwell, The 15 Invaluable Laws of Growth: Live Them and Reach Your Potential, read by John C. Maxwell (Hachette Audio, 2012), Audible ed.

Dweck, Carol, Mindset: The New Psychology of Success, read by Bernadette Dunne (Random House Audio, 2019), Audible ed.

Dweck, Mindset.

Geoff Colvin, Talent Is Overrated: What Really Separates World-Class Performers from Everybody Else, read by Geoff Colvin (Penguin Audio, 2019), Audible ed.

Daniel Coyle, The Talent Code: Greatness Isn't Born. It's Grown. Here's How., read by John Farrell (Random House Audio, 2019), Audible ed.

Coyle, The Talent Code.

Dweck, Mindset.

Dweck, Mindset.

Dweck, Mindset.

Olson, The Slight Edge, 141-144.

Olson, The Slight Edge, 40.

Olson, The Slight Edge, 151.

Conclusion

Suzanne Raga, "17 Quotes from Betty White That Will Make You Love Her Even More," Mental Floss, January 17, 2017, https://www.mentalfloss.com/article/70090/17-quotes-betty-white-will-make-you-love-her-even-more

"Career Change Statistics," Career Change Advice, accessed June 28, 2021, https://careers-advice-online.com/career-change-statistics.html

Linda Kaplan Thaler and Robin Koval, Grit to Great: How Perseverance, Passion, and Pluck Take You from Ordinary to Extraordinary (New York: Crown Business, 2015).

Napoleon Hill, Think and Grow Rich, read by Napoleon Hill Foundation (Nightingale-Conant, 1993), Audible ed.

Og Mandino, "The Scroll Marked I," in The Greatest Salesman in the World (New York: Bantam Books, 1968).

ABOUT THE AUTHOR

Dr. Stephen Crawford is a coach, speaker, consultant, and CEO of a Minneapolis based leadership consulting firm. He is on a mission to help business leaders unlock their full potential. He realized that he could have a greater impact on the community by helping missional companies achieve success by clarifying their message and their focus. Stephen Crawford loved people and started his career serving non-profit organizations providing leadership training and strategic planning. He eventually shifted to the world of business where for the last twelve years he has spoken to tens of thousands of people and coached hundreds of leaders on how to get the very best out of themselves. His obsession with personal and professional growth has caused him to amass dozens of licenses and certifications. His doctorate from Bethel University is in Global and Contextual Leadership which was a program committed to social influence and innovation. Stephen is truly on a mission to change the world by unleashing within people the power of their potential. He lives with his family in Minneapolis where his chief aim in life is to watch his children flourish. You find about more about him and his mission at <u>www.experienceleadership.com</u>

CPSIA information can be obtained
at www.ICGtesting.com
Printed in the USA
LVHW091519041221
705280LV00009B/53/J

9 781665 714761